Mana Pass

LEAP(OF FAITH)

Publisher: Put rukopisa

Book one

Translation from Croatian: Maja Kulej

ISBN 978-953-8344-00-8

CIP number is available in catalog of National and University Library

in Zagreb under number 001060537

Mana Pass

Leap (of faith)

Novel

Put rukopisa

Kutina, 2020.

for Marino, mom and dad's greatest wish

This book was not based on a true story,

but every part of it is real

and all of this did happen

to somebody at some point.

1

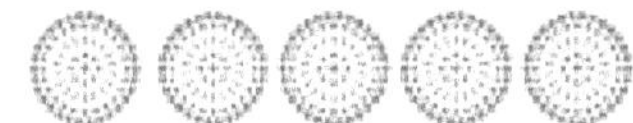

Why haven't I called at least one of them to check if anybody is coming? Because then it wouldn't have been like a scene from a movie screen. Oh well, Nora, now enjoy your movie-like scene while you are standing here all alone in front of the school like an idiot.

Nora was talking to herself while staring at a small pink piece of paper, which very clearly had spent years trying to survive much more than it could. The only thing written on the paper was *10/10/2018 at 6 PM in front of the school*, and it was written ten years ago today.

Since all this had been her idea, she very vividly remembered every detail of that night. It was their first night out after they had gone to college and returned to Kutina for a weekend. As usual, they met at the statue of *Gola Maja*[1], sat on a bench, and started drinking. Yes, on a park bench - like real ladies do. Just the five of them and the stories about what at the time seemed to be the most exciting month of their lives. All of them on their sides of the world with their own adult lives they have been waiting for, for so long. Since they all had gone to different places, Nora decided they had to have something that would forever remain only theirs. So she convinced them to meet at

---

1   Naked Maja

the school in exactly ten years. Nora was not just saying that. No, no. She arrived fully prepared. Each girl got their own piece of paper with the exact date, time, and place of the meetup.

Usually, at least three of the girls from that cheerful group of five would make fun of Nora for trying to pull off the cheesiest moves from the lamest movies ever. They would also laugh at the fact that she brought papers that they were somehow supposed to keep for ten years. And, of course, they would laugh at the fact that those pieces of paper *had* to be pink. Regardless of all that, they knew that they would immediately agree. They were aware, even then, that there were all kinds of families out there, but that theirs was an extraordinary kind.

Led by the belief that alcohol made them more graceful and far more skilled at dancing than usual, they had a lot of fun that night. They were in the best company, and the playlist seemed to be arranged by their wishes. They spent the whole night dancing, jumping, and screaming at every other song the DJ would play. The night ended in front of the bakery, as usual. *Yogurt*[2] and *burek*[3] at 5 AM, after a night out, seemed like the best combination of flavors the human race had ever come up with.

Everyone who was out started gathering in front of the only bakery that was open so early. It was a meeting place where plans about rides home were being negotiated because all the energy you had while clubbing seemed to disappear after you ate something - all of a sudden, you would become incapable of taking two steps. Even if you lived nine minutes away from the bakery, you tried to get into any possible car. That was also the moment when the most crucial thing in the world was to concentrate as hard as you could and try to sound sober for a phone call with your dad, who was supposed to pick you up and take you home. Those three who would ride with you were

2   Balkan Yogurt - set-style yogurt

3   Round filo pastry filled with either cheese, meat, spinach; popular breakfast food in all Balkan countries

wholeheartedly cheering for you in the background. The bakery was also a place where the retelling of everything that had happened that night would begin, and where you would agree on a pretty optimistic wake-up time for a coffee the next day. The next day was not so fun, but why think about that part? After that specific night out, the only thing that mattered was that the small pink pieces of paper were safe in their wallets, with other important documents.

Okay, if nobody arrives by 6:15, I'm going home.

Nora was looking at the school. She stood in front of the entrance and observed the building in which she had spent four unforgettable years. The trees have grown and were drastically giving away the number of years that had passed since the girls had finished the fourth grade[4]. The flowers and shrubs now looked as one had imagined when planting them, and the grass has surrounded the entire school. Everything has changed, but the building remained precisely the same. To Nora, the red bricks, the steps, and the large white columns at the entrance looked just like they did on the first day of school. Even the left entrance to the building was the same - the student entrance, closer to the locker room, where the biggest crowd would gather when the school bus would come. Nora, who used to walk to school because it took her exactly seven minutes, always managed to get there right at that time.

She looked at the windows and realized she still remembered that the chemistry and biology classrooms were upstairs, with the English language and physics classroom beneath them. She remembered the school desk in the middle, where she used to sit. Far enough from the blackboard, and far enough from the back row that was always guilty of something. She also remembered the PE class. The first indication of nice weather equaled running around the school. Or, in her case, walking. Because, firstly, she could run only for 20 meters straight, and secondly, she knew that everyone who had a class at that time was watching her run - because the most exciting thing in the world

---

4   Senior year

while sitting in a classroom was watching those outside running around. Especially when older students had PE. All the girls were, at some point, in love with a boy from the grade up. That was kind of a rule. He had to be cool, he was already older, and he had to be available. Or rather, he had to be someone none of your friends was in love with. That was what it actually meant *to be available* then. And if the universe really worked in your favor, you had an English class at the same time he had PE, and you could watch him without any distraction for the whole period of that class. That situation happened to Nora only one semester, resulting in the worst grades she had ever had in English language. She knew that Saša from the class b[5] was to blame, but she forgave him quickly enough.

*

Dajana found her piece of paper two months before the meetup, but in a hurry, she put it, along with a bunch of other papers, in one of those drawers where you keep absolutely everything. It could have waited there for another ten years, had she not searched for something in that drawer just days before the meetup. She found the small pink paper, remembered that night out, and put it on a fridge. She wondered what the chances of them all coming together were. Slim to none, she thought, but then realized that she would love to see Nora's silly idea work out and for them to see each other after ten years. She thought about the option of calling one of them, but that would not be cool, and she was sure that none of them would do that. Also, she had to think about if she would even be able to take that Wednesday off and go to Kutina.

She just crossed the road going from the cinema to the school and was feeling kind of nervous. She did not know why, but she was excited. Maybe the girls did get together, but who knows what they were like now. In these ten years, she has changed quite a lot. Who

---

5   In Croatian school system students from one grade (e.g. sophomores) are, most often randomly, divided in class departments named a, b, c, etc. *("I go to 1.a class.")*

knows, maybe they have too. And what if they did not all show up? It would not be a big deal, really, but she was already here and would love to see them.

She walked past the store and approached the school, noticing a woman standing by the street lamp right in front of the entrance. The woman was wearing skinny blue jeans, black leather boots with a flat heel, a black knee-length topcoat, a dark blue woolen hat, and the world's most colorful bag. Her blonde, slightly curly, shoulder-length hair was sticking out underneath her hat, which certainly did not serve as a protection against the cold, as it looked more like an accessory. She was looking at the school with her hands in her coat pockets, leaned against the lamp.

- Nora?

*

- I cannot believe that I'm having my ten-year high school reunion already! Are you going to go on yours? – a coworker asked Sofija.

- We are not doing that. I mean, even for the fifth anniversary nobody came forward about it, so I don't think a big ten-year celebration is destined to happen – Sofija passingly explained and continued working, but that question kept going through her head for the entire day. She was wondering about where could all those people from her class be now, but she was really interested in just four of them. She was sorry that they had lost contact, but when she thought about all that had happened to her in the last ten years, she realized how hard contacts are to maintain. At first, they did not give up - they kept trying, but over time too many things took place. It must have been that life happened in the meantime, and everything else was put aside.

They have not been kids for a long time, Sofija thought, but then she remembered something very child-like. Pieces of paper. During her break, she searched through her entire wallet but did not find it. She had not expected to keep it for ten years anyway, but she was annoyed that she could not remember throwing it away. Only that night at home, as she watched some dumb TV show, did she remember that she had put it away with some photographs. She got up from the bed and from her wallet took one of those little paper wraps in which you get your document photos. In it, she kept her own and a bunch of other people's photos. She did not understand why people did that - share their document photos, because, like what, you got too many pictures, so now you had to exchange them with others. Quite strange, but okay.

She found her piece of paper and decided that it was a sign she had to go. It occurred to her to call Nora and ask her if she was going, but she knew that doing that would hurt Nora more than nobody showing up. She was going to Kutina, and if no one else showed up, she would just visit her family. It has been a while anyway.

She made a turn to the street toward the school, and while driving next to it, she saw two people turn their heads after her car. At that moment, she felt an incredible excitement that took her by surprise and made her laugh. She parked at the school and headed toward the girls. She immediately recognized Dajana with her white sneakers, fashionably ripped jeans, plain oversized white T-shirt, and a leather jacket. Her long, straight, brown hair bounced along with her when she realized who is approaching them. Dajana pointed out to Nora that Sofija is coming, and they both walked toward her and hugged her at the same time.

- One by one, huh?

*

It is incredible how 1376 pieces of paper, cards, photos, trash, and everything else that accumulates over time can fall out of one relatively small wallet. It is just as amazing how that always seems to happen when everyone else in the house is asleep, and something like that could wake them up.

Veronika was listening to the silence of the house and, after a few minutes, realized that her clumsiness had not woken anyone up. Since she was not sleepy, she was looking for something to do. She sat on the floor and began to go through everything that had fallen out of her wallet.

Yes. That is what I need to be doing at 4 AM.

She sat on the floor and started. She put trash in one pile. Small pieces of paper and receipts that she told herself a hundred times she would not squeeze into her wallet anymore. But here, there were already 17 pieces of paper on that pile, confirming that she obviously cannot keep such a decision. She skimmed over all the documents she definitely needed and found a small pink piece of paper. At first, it did not occur to her what it was, but then she remembered. She looked at the paper, which, although it was in the late stages of decay, still had readable date and time on it - 10/10/2018 at 6 PM. *Oh, that's in two weeks.*

She started thinking about whether she could go. She reminisced about numerous situations with the girls, especially Nora's excitement that night out when she had proposed her brilliant idea. Veronika remembered the sense of security she had always felt in that group. If someone had told her then that she would lose contact with the girls, she would say they must be joking. At that time, the thought of something like that happening would not even cross her mind. She would love to see the girls again because as long as it had been, they were her childhood. All those stories and feelings you experience for the first time, and only once in your lifetime, she experienced all of that with them.

I guess everything won't fall apart if I go to Kutina for one day...

She knew there and then that she would go, but there was a lot she had to sort out in the meantime. In fact, Nora's face was the crucial factor in deciding to go. She could exactly imagine the disappointment on Nora's face if no one came or, even worse, if all but one girl showed up. And yet, on the other hand, maybe Nora had changed so much that it did not even matter to her anymore. Perhaps *she* will be the one who would not show up. *Oh, sure,* Veronika thought sarcastically, imagining Nora arriving at the school first and anxiously waiting to see who else was coming.

She decided to walk to school. From the Healthcare Center, she began her descent toward the high school. There were some changes, but the feeling of the city was still the same. She noticed there was a new playground in front of the Healthcare Center, and as tall trees surrounded it, it looked charming. She was now close enough to the school to clearly see the three girls standing in front of it. In an instant, she became nervous like a little kid whose mom and dad had finally given them permission to go to the town with their friends. Although she had not seen her in years, she recognized Sofija first. She looked precisely how Veronika imagined she would look. In a high-waisted black skirt and a white shirt with a long, white neckerchief, she looked like a successful businesswoman. Further contributing to that look, there were the red shoes on her feet, a black coat, and a crimson bag on her arm. Her flowing hair looked like she was just coming from a hair salon, but the thing that had not changed was her smile. Veronika spotted Nora and Dajana standing next to her, and she sneaked up behind them as they were talking about one biology class when the teacher was convinced that a woman across the school was watching him through the window.

- Girls, do you have a free period, or are you playing hooky?

*

- I want this one.

- Ema, take whichever you want, I don't care. I am just saying that one won't fit all the rubbish you usually carry in your wallet.

- But look how pretty it is. Here, I'll throw away everything I don't need, and I won't pile up any more rubbish. This wallet deserves it. Because of it, I'm willing to change.

Siniša just shook his head, and Ema headed for the cash register with her new wallet.

- Are we going to go for a coffee?

- Of course not. I have to go home and organize my beautiful new wallet - Ema said, laughing as she said goodbye to Siniša, who had to go back to work anyway but always tried to prolong his break for just one more coffee.

Ema got home, turned on the TV, and warmed up a leftover lasagna she had made yesterday. After she had done everything there was to do around the apartment, she sat down in the living room and started moving things from her old wallet to the new one. In doing so, she came across a small pink piece of paper.

She had it in her hand several times already, she knew where it was, and in these ten years, she just kept moving it around. Now that the date was so close, it was a different feeling. She had not been to Kutina for a long time, she had had a lot of work lately, and mom and dad often visited her, so she did not really have any reason to go home. But now, she actually wanted to go. She got up and went for her cell phone. She would call Dajana to see if she was coming.

Wait, I won't be the only one to call, she decided and put down her phone. She went back to work, and in the end, she just pushed all the stuff from the old wallet into the new one. *Just as I thought, none of this is actually rubbish, and I need all of it in my wallet. That Siniša guy doesn't have a clue.*

She took the train to Kutina so she could do some work on her laptop. The train station reminded her of all the weekends going back to college. Sundays would always be busiest, so the specialized tactic was required to get yourself a seat. As she was going toward the school, she felt nervous. She walked along Railway Street, turned left, and passed the statue of Gola Maja. She remembered Nora acting all smart about that statue on one night out. She had felt that was the right moment to explain how the statue was made by Ivan Sabolić, that the sculpture's actual name was *"Ležeća figura"*[6] and that it had been in Kutina since 1978. The statue had been vandalized several times, but by now, it was a meaningful symbol of the city. That was the point in her story when she was kindly asked to shut up about it on a Friday night.

Ema was thinking about if anybody was going to show up. She was sure of one thing - if no one came, she would never admit that she was at the school. She walked past the cinema and began to descend toward the school. Although the surroundings have changed a bit, it seemed to her that everything was exactly the same. She never thought that someone could love a city, or that *she* could have any feelings for one. But she really did love this one.

When she made the last turn, she could not believe it. All four of them were already standing there. She noticed Veronika explaining something to the girls. A fashion style that was unquestionably hers. Straight, brown hair, just below the shoulders, and striking brown eyes, which would have that special spark whenever she talked about something fun. She wore white *"starke"*[7], jeans and a brown belt, a long-sleeved red top and a short, black, leather jacket. Ema thought that maybe somebody had brought an extra person with them, but as she got closer, she quickly realized that all of the girls were actually there.

- You can't be serious that all of us are actually here!

- I also have a hard time believing it – Sofija said while greeting Ema.

- Well, I was sure that all of us were going to show up – Nora said, laughing and pointing to a very familiar coffee bar across the street.

- Noa?

- Of course.

---

6   *Lying Figure*

7   Croatian slang for Converse sneakers - *Chucks*

They sat at a table in the corner, by the window overlooking the school. From the outside, the coffee shop looked just like it did ten years ago. Everything stayed the same indoors, too, except for the different kinds of beer bottles and cans displayed on the wall. Lights, which were always dimmed, still gave the place where they had spent every free period a unique atmosphere.

There was nobody there, so the waiter approached them immediately. All of them ordered beer except Nora. She would like to have tea.

- You got all of it, right? That would be five beers — Dajana told the waiter, looking at Nora as if she had ordered poison instead of tea. The waiter glanced once more at Nora, but she only sighed in surrender. It was clear to her that she had no choice.

Veronika was still amazed by the height of the trees. It was a tangible sign of the passage of time, and she could not comprehend that it has actually been that long.

- Hey, Veronika, enough with the trees. We get it. It's grown.

- Okay, okay, I just find it fascinating. I mean, look at the one near the lamp. You see, Ema, that one. It was only planted when we finished school.

- Yeah, I see, yes. All those in favor of Veronika not being allowed to mention anything about trees from now on?

They all raised their hands and looked at Veronika.

What happened next is what happens to all real friendships. In that second, ten years of separation, five different cities, different jobs, and completely different lives, were all gone. There were five girls at that table, all feeling like they had just graduated high school yesterday.

2

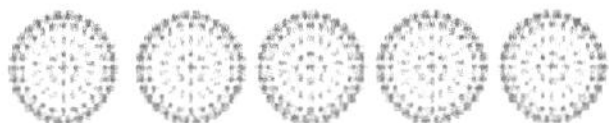

- I can't wait to hear what's new. Nora, go – Dajana said as the ordered beers arrived at the table.

- Why should I be the first one?

- Because all this was your idea, and I think it was one of the better ones – Ema replied, raising her glass to make a toast. They all clinked their glasses and took a sip of cold refreshing beer.

- Oh, so that's the prize? – Nora asked and laughed. She was convinced that the years of separation would have a lot more impact, but some things would never change. Perhaps, at that time, they did not even understand the strength of their bond and the way it connected them and how many people longed to have such lifelong relationships. She was watching them, still not believing that they were sitting together at the table after ten years.

Each of these five women had their own personality, their own way of thinking, their habits, challenges, goals, and opportunities. Dajana was always the motivator, she would never let them get stuck in a routine, and she would always manage to get the group into motion. Ema was the optimist that every group of friends needs, the person who could, in a blink of an eye, find something positive in every situation. Sofija would enchant everyone with her focus, and she was so trustworthy that it was hard to keep anything from her, while Veronika had such an infectious smile, which was equally sincere in any situation, be it fun or sad. Although Nora did not know what had happened to the girls in these ten years, just one look at their faces was enough to tell her that all the important things remained the same. Those things that actually defined them as people were probably the reason they all showed up based on some agreement on a random night out.

- Well, where should I start? And please do not say from the beginning, any of you.

- From Osijek, then. You started college, and I know all the important things that happened thanks to Facebook. I'm interested in everything in between – Ema interjected.

- Yes, you all know about college. That experience was, as it was to all of you, new and exciting and tiring, but it was exactly what I've wanted. I enjoyed the Faculty of Education, and if I had to choose again, I would choose the same – and I guess that's a good sign. There, I met Monika, and the two us quickly became as close as the five of us were in high close. But the whole story of my time in Osijek begins with Viktor.

- Viktor? Oh my, that was the name of that first-grader who was running after Ema for the entirety of our last semester. Remember him? – Veronika said, and they all started laughing. Ema grabbed her head and rolled her eyes. She had entirely forgotten about this boy who would not leave her alone.

- It's not him, is it? – Ema turned in Nora's direction.

- Yes, Ema, it's him. The guy who is three years younger than us, but somehow he ended up in Osijek the same time I did.

- Okay, so it's not him. Just checking. Continue.

- It was the summer after my third year of college. Monika and I decided to go to Kopika[8]. That is a complex of pools close to the Drava river, and it's really cool, especially when the temperature rises to 7000 degrees. There we had our spot, which was available and "ours" precisely two out of 15 times we went there, but whatever. It was perfect. In the shade, but near the area where you can sunbathe, near the pool, and near the playing field where the guys were usually kicking a football. It wasn't jam-packed that day, and Monika even managed to grab the spot under that water mushroom you stand under and get a water massage. I was mostly lying on the grass and reading a book. I had just decided to go into the water when a ball came my way. I noticed three guys looking at me, so I went to kick the ball back to them.

- I'm afraid I can guess how far that ball went – Diana interjected.

- Just a few centimeters, of course. I managed to miss it so much that I lost my balance and fell flat on my face like a pancake. I was so ashamed that I thought about the option of never getting up. Like, act dead, Nora, because not only did you fall like an idiot, but you also had an audience. Monika saw everything from the pool, and still, to this day, she is surprised that she didn't drown of laughter.

- I hope Viktor makes an appearance soon – Ema asked.

- Yes, he leaned over me, took my hand to help me get up, and asked if I was okay. He returned the ball to his friends and turned back to me. Only then did I see how gorgeous he was. Blue eyes, with little wrinkles, the ones you get in the corners of your eyes when you laugh a lot. The high forehead and short, curly, brown hair that was still a little bit damp. A straight nose and a beautiful white smile, leaning a little bit more to one side. He had stubble and a great body. You could tell he was working out, but he didn't have those gym muscles, just beautiful broad shoulders and abs. Out of the blue, he turned around and asked me if he could get my number.

---

8   Copacabana, Osijek

- He asked you that after you fell like that?

- Yeah, he used the situation to his advantage.

*

- Seriously? This spectacle made you ask for my number?

- Definitely. I have decided to be a football manager, so I should always be on a lookout for new talent.

Nora laughed at his joke, which was everything but funny, and if Viktor did not look the way he did, she would probably be more aware that it was a cheesy pick-up line.

- I have to think about if I'm ready to sign the contract.

- Okay, if I can't get your number, will you and your friend at least get a drink with us?

Monika just got back to her towel, still laughing her butt off. She confirmed, on both of their behalfs, that they would join them for drinks. After a couple of football jokes at Nora's expense, which she did not understand, but they were supposedly funny, the atmosphere was great. They started to order drinks, and Nora was talking to Viktor the whole time. She liked his way of thinking. He had an opinion about everything but did not act like there was no chance he could be wrong. He seemed calm and mysterious and attractive, and like everything a boy who you just started to like should be. Besides, Nora liked him so much that it was quite apparent to her that every other word she said might sound ludicrous, but she could not help herself.

Drinking at a bar soon turned to a night out. They went to a club that was so crowded it seemed as if half of the town was there. By some miracle, they managed to find a free table, which Monika and Nora immediately occupied while the boys were getting drinks. When the speaker right next to that table began to literally bounce from the sound volume, it became clear to them why it was available. The club was so full you could barely pass through all the people. You could only dance, that is, move to the rhythm of everybody else moving. The good thing was you could not fall even if you wanted to. And the second good thing was that Nora was right next to Viktor the entire time they were dancing. She could smell his perfume, which mingled with the smell of chlorine from the pool, but, like everything else about Viktor, it completely overwhelmed her. The moment he moved towards her like he was about to kiss her, Nora looked at Monika and saw that the situation was not great. Monika's usually neatly done hair was now in her face, and she looked like she was fighting with it. The right sleeve of her loose dark-purple shirt was drenched, and her green eyes were half-shut.

Nora went to her and started getting her ready for going home. Viktor asked if they need a ride, but Nora said it was okay. He asked for her phone number again. She looked at him and asked him to give her his phone.

*

Monika woke up around noon. She walked out of the room in an oversized T-shirt she slept in, with her mascara smudged and hair so messy it looked like it would never go back to normal. She looked at herself in the hallway mirror and made a face as if she had seen a monster. The shape of her face perfect for smiling. She had beautiful white teeth, rosy cheeks, and small eyes that would close every time she laughed. All the lines on her face seemed like they were there because of the laughter, which was probably right. She had never used too much make-up or dressed up, and the only jewelry she accepted were the three bracelets she wore – leather straps with a pendant in the middle, and a plain hand-knitted bracelet which loosened up and went up to her elbow, making Monika panic thinking she lost it. At that moment, she swore that she would never, but never, taste alcohol again. Then she switched to Nora and started complaining about how she could let her drink so much. She decided that a real friend would not do that. Of course. And then she remembered.

- Oh my God, yes! The reason you let me drink so much is you were talking to Viktor the whole night. I want to know everything, talk.

- Ugh, I don't know, Monika.

- Come on, don't make excuses. What do you mean, you don't know?

- He's great. I don't know. I had never met anyone who I could immediately talk to so easily. He is so interesting and funny. And the fact that he is handsome doesn't hurt either.

- He is really attractive, I admit. Interesting? I wouldn't know because we didn't talk much. But, Nora, I have to tell you that he really wasn't that funny – Monika teased her because she realized right away that Nora really liked him. And when you as a friend realize that, you get the exclusive right to tease.

- I really want to know what is wrong with him…

- Excuse me?

- Well, he doesn't have a girlfriend. Don't you find that weird?

- I don't. I don't have a boyfriend either, and I am the most normal person on the planet. Ever.

- Monika, yesterday you were explaining the difference between blue and navy blue. To a guard.

- But I'm not even sure I know the difference.

- Exactly. You don't.

- Well, anyway. I hope you gave him your number.

- I did, but he hasn't called yet. He's probably not going to, but fine, whatever. I still had fun.

- I love that "whatever". It's probably the biggest lie ever. Okay, we give him the right to call until the end of the day. After that, we don't love him anymore.

- Deal.

They started watching a movie, and Monika fell asleep in ten minutes. During the commercials, Nora reflexively picked up her phone, as usual. She had just unlocked it when it started ringing. Unknown number. She kicked Monika, who jumped half asleep, all confused.

- Monika, Monika, Monika! I think it's him, what should I do???

- Ha? Wait, wait? Who? What? – Monika tried to understand what was happening, and with a half-open eye, she saw the phone pushed in her face.

- Oh, you silly fool. Well, answer it! – she said sarcastically, considering it was the only thing Nora could do, besides not picking up, which would be stupid.

Nora tried to get herself together for a second, and then she answered. It was him. He said that he hoped she had a good night's sleep and that Monika was feeling better. He asked her if tomorrow was a good time to pick her up. In those words. Like it was not even a question of whether or not they would go, he just wanted to know when. Nora said that tomorrow was fine, so they agreed he would pick her up around 2 PM. And that was that.

- He asked about me? Either the boy knows the game, or he's just really nice – Monika concluded wisely.

Nora left Monika alone with her hangover and went to finish everything she had to do for college, so she could have tomorrow completely free. That was her plan, but her thoughts were with Viktor. She was excited and could not wait for tomorrow to come. She remembered that feeling when she was a kid. The feeling when you could not wait for the night to come so you could go to sleep and wake up as soon as possible because of some exciting thing that day. The next day she was next to Monika's bed at 9 AM, trying to wake her up.

- Monika, come on. I made coffee, please get up and help me get dressed. I have absolutely nothing to wear. I should just call Viktor and let him know I can't go anywhere because I have no clothes. None.

- First thing, it's 9 in the morning, Nora, and you go at 2 PM. At 2! That is in, like, I don't know, a lot of hours. And secondly, by making that kind of statement, that you are always naked, you could create a pretty wrong picture of yourself.

They spent the next two hours trying to match all the pieces of clothing in that apartment to make Nora look exactly right for her first date. The outfit had to be cute, but also comfortable because, along with the general stress about the date, Nora could not handle having to also worry about the way she had to sit down or stand up or something similar. The additional problem was his ambiguity about where they were going. After the fashion police session and all the clothes spread out in the living room, hallway, kitchen, bathroom, and bedroom, and all the combinations they went through, Nora decided on skinny dark jeans, sneakers, and a colorful shirt. That was actually the first combination she tried on a few hours ago.

Viktor was not late. He waited for her in front of the building, leaned against his car. He was wearing sneakers, jeans, and a burgundy T-shirt. The first thing Nora noticed was the smile. Fine lines appeared around his eyes when he saw her, and that made her feel so much better. She just had to say "hey" casually, and that was that. Everything else would be fine.

- Hey.

- Well, hey, Nora. You look great, perfect for where we are going.

- And that would be...

- A surprise.

And here they were again. Again those smiling eyes. As Nora was sitting in the car, she realized that this smile could cost her a lot. Even though she had always been a hopeless romantic, she never actually believed something like that would happen in real life. It was a fun idea, but obviously not conceivable. She still believed that, but now there was this boy who she liked more than she was used to. All those typical doubts and female theories started going through her head. *Okay, you like him, but calm down a bit. There's a good chance he doesn't like you to the same extent, so you better keep it cool. There is also a big chance that he is actually a jerk or a psychopath, given that you only met him two days ago, and you can't really know him.*

They drove for about ten minutes. During that time, Viktor was asking her about her day. They talked about their night out and everything that happened after the girls left. He told her how they missed the best drunken hamburgers that no one dares to eat sober, but that nothing else worth mentioning happened. She explained that she might not know much about Osijek, but she knows about the *trovač*[9]. It was a tradition of Osijek's nightlife – every student had to end up there at some point. They got out of the car, and Nora realized they were at the city stadium.

- I worry about you and my paycheck if I become your manager, so I figured we should work on your free kicks a little bit – Viktor said as he threw a football from the trunk her way. She laughed and followed him to the entrance. Despite all the romantic movies she had analyzed over the years, he managed to surprise her.

They entered the stadium, and after dropping his backpack to the grass, he took Nora's hand and led her to the goal. He put the ball down and started playing a goalkeeper.

- So, the first lesson. Don't step on the ball. It goes a lot farther if you kick it.

- You're some jokester, huh?

She got into position and miraculously managed to kick the ball,

---

9   The poisoner – a nickname of the locally famous street vendor that sells fast food (Jozo Trovač)

which went all the way to the goal. She did not score, but, for her, this was good enough. They were kicking the ball at the goal for a while, and Nora had a great time. She enjoyed laughing and playing something that looked like football to her, but to any reasonable person, it would have probably looked like a children's game. Nora lay down on the grass and closed her eyes while Viktor went to the other side of the field to get the ball. Soon, he lay down beside her. She could feel the grass under her back, the sun on her face, and the smell of Viktor's perfume. She was watching the clouds, slowly getting that dizzy feeling you get when clouds start to move faster. While observing the stadium, she wondered how come Viktor could just walk in here. The seats were mostly blue, but the white ones were used to write out the words across the stands. On one side, it was written "NK Osijek"[10], and on the opposite side, "Grad na Dravi."[11] A running track surrounded the entire field, and the size of the stadium was breathtaking. It must have been an incredible feeling to play or score a goal in front of so many people. It was undoubtedly just as intense to miss a goal in front of so many people. Nora decided she could never be an athlete.

- That's it? Did I win?

- Not a chance. It's only a half-time. Do you even know the rules of football?

- No, obviously.

- It doesn't matter, that's why we're here.

Viktor laughed at her joke and went to get his backpack while Nora sat up and watched after him. He had that sporty way of running. She did not know what exactly that meant, but it looked good. She was grateful to him for making her feel relaxed. At that moment, she noticed she had stopped thinking. When you are a woman with hundreds of ideas, questions, and situations running through your

---

10   FC Osijek (football club)

11   City on the Drava

mind all the time, the possibility of not having to think is the best thing that can happen.

- I have prepared a luxurious lunch that you will remember for the rest of your life – he stood in front of her like a TV weatherman and began to pull things out of his backpack.

- We start with red wine, vintage 1934. Also known as the year when grapes gave the maximum yield. Have a taste, please.

- Yeah, great aroma. It's interesting how red wine can taste so much like ordinary cherry juice.

- Yes, that is interesting. We continue with an entree. Crackers baked on low heat, so they retain all the nutrients. They were baked like that for three days and three nights, and then subsequently cooled in the moonlight.

- VIC crackers.[12] Awesome! – Nora got excited and took the pack from Viktor's hand.

- And now for the main course. By her accent, we can detect that this young lady is not from Slavonia[13], so I've decided to present her the best of our cuisine – *kulenova seka*[14].

Viktor pulled out two sandwiches and handed one to Nora. He sat down next to her and started eating. They talked about her college experience, what interests her in children's education, and how she was getting used to Osijek. He spoke of his parents and working with them. They were getting to know each other through the information that everyone would consider basic, even banal, but when told by someone you like, it was of greater value. She was feeling great, relaxed, and happy. They spent three and a half hours at the stadium without Nora even noticing that so much time had passed.

12   Popular Croatian brand of crackers

13   One of four Croatian regions, located on the very north-east of Croatia, with Osijek as its largest city

14   A variety of kulen sausage, literally translated *kulen's little sister*

They slowly packed things in his backpack and headed to the car. He got out of the car in front of her building to say goodbye and ask her if she would like to hang out again. Of course, she said yes. One afternoon was enough for her to decide he was not a jerk or a psychopath, and it seemed like she had also made him laugh, so he must have liked her. He got close to her, gently grabbed her face with his hands, and kissed her before she even knew what was happening. Considering how nervous she was, that was probably the best move he could have done. She could feel herself trembling in his hands, the feeling she had never experienced before, and it was incredible. They said goodbye, and she walked into the building with the biggest smile in the world.

She was thinking about the feeling he managed to evoke in her. It was wonderful that he did something as romantic as bringing her to that stadium. He impressed her with everything, from what he did and said, to the way he acted. She felt like actually being in one of her romantic movies, and she did not care what anybody had to say about that. That feeling really existed, and now she had experienced it too.

When she heard the door, Monika jumped from the bathroom to the hallway. Nora looked at her, leaning against the door, with a smile on her face that she could not wipe away even if she wanted to. If someone told her the worst news in the world at that moment, she would probably still just smile.

- You are done, huh?

- I'm afraid I am.

3

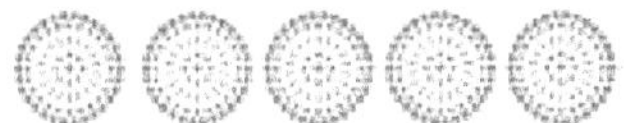

Nora was lying in bed and did not feel like opening her eyes. She hated Thursdays. No other day of the week could be as awful as a Thursday. The week was already going on for long enough that she was exhausted, but the weekend was still far away. But the crucial factor was that, on Thursdays, absurd and unbelievable things would often happen to her, coincidentally or not. For example, today, she had to go to the library and ask if she could take home a book that she needed to write her master's thesis. And she knew that the grumpy red-headed hag would be working that day, the one that used her dragon powers to destroy all the students who even tried to set foot on the holy ground of the library. One could never imagine that her job actually was to loan those books to them.

The smell of the coffee made Nora smile. Monika obviously woke up before her. Nora looked at the clock and saw that it was only 6:30 AM, which meant she had a few hours left until her class. As she sat on the bed and took a deep breath, her lips spread into a grin. Every Thursday, Viktor would take her out to a lot of cake and ice-cream to brighten her day, which she so unfairly declared as the worst. He said that everybody knew that there was nothing worse than a Monday. Sometimes, he was really silly... She swiftly slipped on her slippers and ran to the kitchen.

- Good morning. I'm not even going to ask how you are. I know what day it is – Monika was already waiting for her, with Nora's sizeable red coffee cup ready.

- Ah... Aren't you just a sight for sore eyes on days like these – Nora laughed, holding the cup with both hands.

- Firstly, you are drinking too much coffee. Nobody owns a mug as large as yours. And secondly, I no longer believe you don't like Thursdays. Ever since you've been with Viktor, I think you can't wait for a Thursday to come because he treats you like a princess, you manipulator. In fact, I think all of it was just your evil trick and that I'm onto you, finally.

- Of course, your wisdom is unmatched – Nora stuck her tongue out at Monika like a little kid.

- Whatever, coffee is a must for every self-respecting person, thank you very much. There is something important I wanted to talk to you about.

- Yes? – Monika looked at Nora suspiciously while taking a big sip of the aromatic beverage.

- I would like to negotiate your yellow dress – Nora immediately raised her right hand to silence her friend.

- Before you object, please listen to my arguments. So, think about it as an investment for your peaceful afternoon you would otherwise spend wandering around in search of clothes for me, as it usually happens. Second, I have to be pretty for my boyfriend, while you for your cat on the couch, not so much. Third, that dress really fits me... Which does not mean it doesn't fit *you*... And yes, the last thing, today is a Thursday, and I really don't like Thursdays and need something to cheer me up – she was batting her eyelashes dramatically to point out her sad face.

- I'm not Viktor, so your sad puppy eyes won't work on me. And who says I don't have to be pretty for the cat. When he sees you in the morning, with your messy hair and your torn pajamas, he doesn't recover from the shock until we get back from our classes. Look at him, he's still under the couch, afraid to come out, poor thing – she sniffled at the cat, urging him to sit on her lap.

- So we have a deal – Nora clapped her hands and put the cup in the sink. She passingly kissed Monika and, slamming the bathroom door, loudly thanked her. Monika just shook her head, laughing.

In the shower, Nora was thinking about how eager she actually was to see him, kiss him, talk to him. In fact, he was the reason she started to love those nights, which became their tradition. First, they would walk around the city, and then they would go to the lousiest cake shop in the whole Osijek. The first time he took her there, she could not stop worrying about getting salmonella. Until she tried the cakes. They were the most wonderful thing she had ever tasted. Perfectly balanced flavors, very soft sponges, and full-flavored creams. They were like the cake made by your grandma when she really wanted to cheer you up. Viktor said that the cake shop had been around as long as he could remember. The owners were an older married couple who had inherited the shop from some uncle. There was not a huge variety of thousand cakes and ice cream flavors, but what they did have was divine. The two of them would always sit right next to the window overlooking a not-so-busy street – a few cars here and there, mostly children running to the playground, and an odd couple in love hiding out on the side streets. The chairs they were sitting on were old, with large and thick green cushions. The backrests were made of flower-shaped wrought iron, just like a small round table that could barely fit everything they had ordered. The whole place had a vintage ambiance, furnished with some antique lanterns and lamps that did not give enough light to illuminate the entire room. But that was the magic of it. The environment was so homey, intimate, and familiar, that she fully understood his fascination with the place. She would usually order Irish cream and eat pistachio cake, as well as strawberry-orange cake. That day, she was thinking about how she could really use a double dose of something very chocolatey. She loved the fact that, in front of him, she did not have to hold back or feel ashamed. They came here with a mission to drown themselves in sugar, so that was exactly what would happen. And if he thought that she did hold back and was not eating enough, he would try to feed her himself, which would always be hilarious and embarrassing at the same time.

Nora made it to her class at the last minute and crawled into a seat in the back of the classroom. This lecture was not something that interested her, nor was it necessary for her, so she decided to spend those two hours to work on her thesis. In fact, she was so stoked about her topic that she would spend every waking hour mulling over it. It was something that did not give her rest, compelling her to dig and research. She wanted to find as many examples and specific cases from the practice. She made notes and underlined all the professional texts she could find. She was lucky that her professor and his assistant really came through and provided a bunch of literature that could help her. They were surprised as well, not only by her interest but also by her knowledge in the field of behavioral disorders in children. She got interested in it even before she enrolled in college, by reading a book The Spark by Kristine Barnett, which might have been the key factor in deciding which college she should go to. Nora believed that it was possible to bring out the best from every behavioral disorder, as long as you recognize every child's potentials and interests. Exactly that interpretation gave her a lot of extra points with the professor, who then found it easy to invest in a student who clearly understood the issue and wanted to change something. In agreement with him, she started working on her master's thesis. She was now at the part about children with ADHD and their defiance to the surroundings. She used a red highlighter to angrily underline everything she did not agree with, finishing that text just as the lecture was over. For a moment, she felt guilty for not paying attention, but she got over it quickly. The lecture was held by a professor who, they suspected, could possibly be a vampire, considering how old he was. He was teaching every generation that was ever recorded. Nobody had ever heard of this subject being thought by anybody else. And the lecture was the same way – the same for 46 years, approximately. Monika gave herself the liberty to not even show up. Talk about model students.

- But that is totally frustrating! If I were a parent, I wouldn't let it pass! It's unbelievable that for years science has been trying to explain it in that way. Wherever I find a connection of ADHD with defiance to surroundings, everyone is defining it as a reflection of the family's value system and broken family relationships. That makes it seem like every one of those children came from a problematic environment. I don't agree with that, a child is seeking their autonomy, just like any of us, and if that is not acknowledged and that child is persistently pushed into for them uncomfortable situations, isn't it logical for them to be defiant? I mean, in which way can they even demonstrate their disagreement? If their interests are recognized in time, and God knows there is a multitude of possibilities to do that, a child will invest their energy in those things that appeal and are important to them, as we all do. It hurts my heart to think of all those children that possibly have a little genius for drawing, writing, math, or modeling hiding inside, and nobody sees that. Instead, they are pushed into social interactions, mundane classes of general knowledge, writing, reading, or something else. Those things have to be mastered too, of course, but the important part is that thing that will pull them in! That has to be ferreted out and well-polished, and then everything else will fall into place.

- You are gorgeous when you get excited about something. I could watch you for hours, just talking about what you love – Viktor played with her hair.

- And you know, what you're saying makes a lot of sense. But I think it demands a lot of time, energy, and determination. I am not sure how much time do teachers have or even if they want to do it.

- Yes, that is the main problem. I think a special college major should be introduced, one that would guide us specifically in that direction. Even though it's a narrow scope, I believe that there would be a great response and, in the end, great results.

- Possibly, but you do know that here everyone thinks only about the profitability. Have you talked to your professor about it? — he switched their plates. Viktor ate half of his pistachio cake and was ready to start her chocolate one, which earned him a slap on the wrist.

- Leave that, I need all the chocolate I could get. And I did, I was pleasantly surprised. He said that he agrees with me and that he wishes more students would approach him with such zeal and enthusiasm. He feels those are the people that will bring change. I was as proud as a peacock — she laughed and dug into her cake. It was a hazelnut and chocolate cake, with parfait cream and light sponge with rum. It was like an explosion of flavors melting in her mouth. She wanted to eat four pieces, or maybe eat until she burst, it was that good.

- Of course, he praised you! You're perfect, and you're mine, is there a better combination? — he smiled at her like a schoolboy in love, and all that went through her head was how on earth is she ever going to be angry at him.

After dessert, they went for a walk around the city. The night was fresh, and it was exactly what Nora needed. She knew that she would have to spend the following days working hard on her thesis. But that did not bother her much because she could not wait to get home and, with fresh coffee, get on her computer.

Viktor adored his city, and Nora loved listening to him talk about it. He knew a lot about Osijek's history; he had researched it all his life and knew how to convey that special feeling he had towards this city. The first thing Nora learned about Osijek from him was about the greenery, which was everywhere. He told her there are 17 parks in total and that Osijek was the city with the largest number of green areas in Croatia. That night they had walked the familiar route, and it began on the Promanada[15]. Nora loved walking along the Drava river, especially at night, when the pedestrian bridge looked magical. There was always somebody walking, running, or cycling on the pathway filled with benches, tall lamps, and plants.

- How many people, do you think, pass through here over during the weekend?

- I have no idea, like 3,000.

- Pff, I'd say at least 10,000 – Viktor said and went quiet.

- And the correct number is?

- I haven't got a clue.

- Great info, thank you – Nora said with that silly, in-love smile that she still could not get rid of. Viktor loved that. He loved watching her, and he was in love with every inch of her face, her green eyes, and blond wavy hair. She had an honest smile and the cutest nose in the world, based on his personal opinion, at least. Her style was totally quirky, but, on her, it all somehow made sense. Nora remembered him telling her about her beloved bridge the first time they had gone for a walk. He explained that the bridge had been built in 1981 and that it was 35 meters high, but that it did not always look like this.

It had been renovated several times over the years, mostly because of the damage caused by the War.[16] She wanted to seem smart and informed, so she asked him to take her to the Youth Bridge as well, which made him laugh so hard that she wanted to push him in the Drava. When he calmed down, he told her that that was the same bridge. It was just the old name which some people still used. She said that she already knew that, and that she was just testing him.

____

15   The promenade in Osijek along the Drava
16   Croatian War of Independence

Viktor's favorite part of the city was King Tomislav Park. It was the biggest park in Osijek, and it looked beautiful at any time of the year. Well-tended paths, lots of trees, and green grass were just perfect for recharging your batteries. It was nice to just walk through the park in silence and enjoy the smell of the leaves and the view of old Baroque Tvrđa.[17]

- Do you know there is a reason they built so many parks around Tvrđa?

- So that Tvrđa could feel nice and cozy?

- Yes, of course, that is the obvious one. But besides that, the Upper and Lower Town had to be moved one kilometer from the fortress walls because that was the range of the cannons. So, the parks were the easiest way to do that.

Whenever they walked around there, Nora would insist they go see *Fićo* and the tank. To her, that was the most fascinating attraction. She would also ask Viktor to repeat the same story every time.

- This is an installation set up to commemorate a specific event dating back to Homeland War.[18] It happened on the 27th of June 1991, when tanks were raging on the streets of the city. Branko Breškić tried to stop them by parking his red Fiat in the middle of an intersection...

- *Fićo*.

- Yes, *Fićo*. One of the tanks ran over *Fićo* and crushed it into pieces. That is why they had placed this installation of a small red *Fićo,* running over a big grey tank, right at this place.

They were holding hands, and he was gently caressing her with his fingers. Both of them in their own world, but it was enough that they were together. Even when they were not talking, they had an exceptional understanding of each other's needs. They walked

---

17   The 18th century Baroque fortress

18   Another name for Croatian War of Independence

towards the parking lot and passed the popular Osijek's Šetač.[19] It was a two-meter high bronze statue of the writer August Cesarac, which was, Nora learned from Viktor, the first street sculpture in Croatia, set up in 1974. He was so popular that at one point they put his silhouette on traffic lights, instead of those little human figures which show when you can cross the road.

- Hello, Šetač – Nora said and waved to the statue.

- I wish he would reply to you one time, so I could see you run for the hills – said Viktor, laughing.

She was breathing in the fresh air, not believing she was so lucky and that she was doing so well. Viktor walked her to the front door where they said goodbye, and when she walked into the house, Monika was waiting for her in the living room, eating ice cream straight out of the box.

- Good evening. That mess you left is still waiting for you in my room – Monika grinned, and Nora instantly felt ashamed. She really did make a mess and had every intention of cleaning it up, but she was in a hurry, and Viktor was already waiting for her.

- I brought you these two cakes to redeem myself, but as far as I can see, you already had your fair share of something sweet – Nora leaned in and kissed Monika on the cheek, then jumped on the bed next to her. Monika was writing an essay on her laptop.

- There is no such thing as too much sweet. Thank you, I will need it because I'm planning to stay up all night to finish this – Monika already unpacked a little green bag with the cakes.

- Great! Me too! I'm going to make some coffee and join you. I managed to persuade the dragon lady to allow me to take the book home. But she said I could have it only until tomorrow, so I have to take out all of the quotes I need right now!

____

19   The Walker

- Coffee... Wonderful. Which book did you take?

- Winkel's *Schwierige Kinder - Problematische Schuler,*[20] the professor recommended it to me. He says that every teacher should read it, even if they don't deal or work exclusively with such children. It is, supposedly, full of real-life examples, and I think I could use a lot of it in my paper. Besides that, I hope it can help me with my professional orientation.

- Yes, I've heard about that book, I just don't understand why don't they give it out of the library. It's not just some little book you can read in an hour or two.

- Allegedly, someone has stolen the other copy, so this is the only one they have. Do you want some sugar in your coffee?

- A spoonful. I can imagine that woman raging when you asked her. How come she gave it to you in the end? She never usually allows it to anyone.

- It was tough, I had to bribe her with a chocolate bar and tell her a professor was sending me — Nora smirked as she poured coffee into two huge cups.

- You will go bankrupt even before you graduate. You can't bribe everyone with chocolate — Monika laughed as Nora handed her coffee.

- Hey look, you gotta do what you gotta do. It will all pay off — Nora chuckled and pulled out her precious book.

It was after 3 AM when they were both ready for bed. Monika finished the essay, while Nora had written out five A4 pages on both sides. The papers were full of different colors because she was a visual type. Highlighters in all possible shades, as well as little sticky labels to mark the most important parts, were crucial. It had gotten to the point that she even had ballpoint pens in different colors. Her college

---

20   Free translation: *Difficult Children – Problematic Students*

girlfriends were always appalled by the riot of colors they would experience while reading her notes. Their claim was that their brains could not determine what was important and what not because everything was too highlighted. But they did not have a system. In Nora's head, everything was in order and made total sense. The more beautiful she found a specific color, the more relevant the information was, and that made her pay more attention to it. Now she was looking through her papers. There were a lot of cases, written down in her tiny handwriting, as well as some suggestions from renowned pedagogues and pediatric psychologists on how to solve them. The colors were everywhere, and she was pleased with the amount of information she had gathered in those few hours, which had flown right by. She packed everything she found in a folder and left it on a kitchen table so she would not forget to bring it to college. Tomorrow, her professor had office hours, and she was bringing him the first part of her thesis for a review. She wanted to, at the same time, present how she imagined the second part should look like. At this point, she was dead tired, so she skipped a late-night shower and postponed it for the morning. Before bed, she glanced at her phone, which lit with a green light, indicating a message. Viktor wished her sweet dreams with a dramatically cheesy text, which made her melt. She was a hopeless romantic, and he knew it. Replaying now was a bad idea because she knew he had work in the morning. But even if it was not, it was so late that she instantaneously fell asleep, cradling her phone.

An irritating alarm that Monika was not turning off awakened Nora. Her yelling from her room did not seem to help, so Nora was forced to get up and physically deal with that temptress. When she glanced at the clock, she realized it was her time to get up too, so she quickly stuffed a sandwich in her mouth, almost choked, and washed it down with a few sips of coffee to make it go down smoother. She threw on a denim jacket and picked up the bag essentials, rushing to meet with the professor. When she called Viktor on her way there, he acted offended for a few minutes because she had not replied last night. But after she promised to go with him to a football match next weekend and treat him with kebab and beer, he yielded. *God, there is nothing a woman can't do with a man who has a weakness for food and football, the sky is the limit* – she thought, dying from laughter. The phone started ringing in her bag as soon as she put it away. She was frantically digging through the bag; she had found a lipstick, an eyeshadow, a pair of spare socks, a handful of suspiciously soft candy, but the phone was nowhere to be found. It is incredible how this evil thing manages to hide just when one needs it the most. Just when she had a desperate thought that she would have to stop and dump everything from the bag out in the middle of the street, she managed to scrape it out with her fingertips.

- Hello? – she shouted breathlessly into the phone.

- Hello, love? How are you? – her mom chirped from the other end.

- Hey, mother! I'm just on my way to college. I'm fine, you? How's dad? – as soon as Nora heard her mother's voice, her mood immediately improved.

- We're all right, I just miss you, so I wanted to hear your voice.

- I miss you both a lot, too. I might come home next weekend. It all depends on my progress with the thesis.

- I was just about to ask you, how is that going?

- Well, I'm satisfied. I've finished more than half of it. I've just arrived in front of the faculty building, I'm going to the consultation. I'll get back to you later. Give dad a kiss from me.

- All right, love, talk to you later. Good luck – Nora hung up and shoved the phone back in the bag, hoping she would find it quicker the next time.

It was a minute before 9 AM when she knocked on the professor's door. When she heard „*Come on in!*" she squeezed through the door that would not open all the way. Every time she would go through them, she could not help but wonder how do heftier people come in. Behind the door, this dude kept boxes of papers and books, which he had probably had since the Middle Ages. He had the messiest office of all the professors she had been to. In there, you first had to make room on a chair so you could sit, not to mention the desk that had an old typewriter on it, which he certainly did not use, seeing as next to it was a functioning computer. The professor was short and balding. He always wore suits with interesting checkered patterns, which were quite obviously out of style. In all likelihood, he was wearing the same ones for the last thirty years. That day, he wore a light yellow shirt, a dark green jacket, and pants with large yellow and brown squares. If anyone else had worn the same outfit, it would be awful and tasteless, but when on him, it seemed quite natural, like it was made for him. He turned from the closet and smiled from ear to ear. His joy was infectious. He was a favorite professor to most of his students because he was bursting with positive energy, had a lot of understanding, and was never in a bad mood or angry.

- Good morning, colleague![21] How are we today? – he rushed to the table to make room for her to write and sit. He began to toss papers from one pile to another. God, he was messy.

- Good morning. It's a beautiful day, so I can't feel bad, and you? – he cleared only half of the chair for her. For a moment, she just looked at it confused, but as he motioned for her to sit, she sat down, resting only on half of her butt.

- I'm always great, especially when students with whom I can have constructive discussions come in – he laughed and sat down opposite her.

- Let's take a look at what you have brought me.

- The first part of the thesis is done – she handed him the folder.

---

21   Translator's note: At Croatian universities and schools, there is a practice of everybody addressing each other with a term *colleague*, as a sign of mutual respect of fellow members of a specific profession

- And for the rest, I thought only to use the cases from practice. I read the book you recommended, and I would like to use it as the base. I would refer to their examples, but I want to compare them or theoretically apply them to our educational and preschool cases. I would go to several schools, I had already contacted some teachers, and I would try to identify, on certain types of behavioral disorders, what are the things a particular child is good at, and what would inspire them to give 110 percent. Because I know that they can and have the potential to do so. Every child has it. Like all of us.

- Great idea! I have also found contact information from some of my former students who encountered this diagnosis in their work; it might not be a bad idea for you to inquire about some of their examples. But I'm certainly delighted with your concept of doing the practical part, as most students avoid it and settle for basically transcribing the literature and combining five or six authors, which they later cite as sources. Have you thought about how to approach these children?

- Yes, I've thought about it. Of course, the teachers know their kids the best, and they should be able to recognize their affinities. I made quick card games and asked the teachers to hand them out to the whole class, not only to that child, so that they wouldn't feel different from the start. I hope that through these games, I can identify their interests. I covered drawing, writing, music, math, and modeling, or handcraft. So in every game, I aim for all of this, but I give priority to only one through their answers. When I cover more games, I should be able to recognize the pattern. I hope. I know this is just a rough take and not quite enough, but I think it will be interesting for a start.

- I agree; the idea of games at that age is phenomenal. A child, thinking that they are just playing games, will, in fact, show what he or she is most fond of. Great idea, colleague. I see that you don't even need me – he laughed at loud, with his stomach bouncing over his tight pants.

- Of course, I do. If you hadn't directed me to the right literature,

I wouldn't have developed such ideas myself — she smiled and waited for him to flip through the first part of her paper. It took him about ten minutes, and in that time, Nora studied the collection of children's literature that adorned the sidewalls of the room. It was truly impressive. Along with all the titles she was familiar with, there were many, at least three times as many, of those that were unfamiliar to her. There is no doubt that a collection like that had been in works for years.

- I am incredibly pleased, colleague, I would suggest very few corrections. When you include your practical part, I can safely say you are ready to defend your master's thesis!

Nora almost burst with pride.

4

She was not ready! She was everything but ready. She stood in front of a massive mirror in the hallway, staring at herself and hissing, which was some miserable imitation of deep breathing to calm herself down. She wore black pants and a light blue shirt with a dark blue print of swallows in flight. On her feet, she had plain black flats, and her hair was neatly combed and pinned with black bobby pins all around.

- You look like a nerd – Monika told her in passing. Nora was obviously in a complete state of shock because she was incapable of any kind of plausible response, except something that sounded awfully like a gurgle. Monika walked back to her and stood just behind her, looking at their reflections in the mirror.

- For God's sake, you look like you're going to faint. You look horrible – she took Nora by the hand and sat her down at the kitchen table. Nora still had a weird *I'm-currently-dying* look in her eyes.

- Heeey! Come on, drink some water, and get yourself together. What came over you? – Monika shoved a glass of water and a row of chocolate in Nora's hands.

- Your thesis defense is not for another two hours. If you continue to hyperventilate like this, you're going to end up in an emergency room even before it starts.

- I don't think I've ever had this kind of jitters in my life... - Nora whimpered, swallowing whole cubes of chocolate.

- I can see that. Calm down, woman, you know everything. You've been working on it for six months now, and there's nothing that could surprise you. I will even be so bold and say you know more about this topic than the professor himself. You'll be great, sweetie! – Monika smiled at her and opened the window to let the fresh air in. All of that – the air, water, and chocolate – seemed to had had some effect. The brain stopped threatening with overheating, legs with giving out, and lungs with exploding.

- Who did you call a nerd?!

- And just like that, you're back – Monika slapped her across her back.

- Come on, then, on your feet! Let's go and get what you've been waiting for all these grim college years!

For the fifth time, Nora checked to see if she had put the USB in her bag and if she had a copy of her thesis and gifts for professors ready. With shaky hands, she flipped through the pages of her paper, reading the examples that she already knew by heart. Even the order they were in. Monika was right; it was impossible she did not know something. She was ready; in fact, she was more than ready – this was the thing she wanted to do in life, there was no way she could screw it up. *Everything will be fine!* She had been repeating that sentence for a good fifteen minutes when the doorbell rang. Viktor walked into the room. Tall and blonde as he was, in a formal dark blue suit, he looked like a model who had just come to take a break from filming an advertisement for an expensive brand of men's suits. The smell of his perfume flooded the room instantly. Nora adored the combination of citrus and some sweet note that she had never recognized. It was her favorite men's cologne, and it suited Viktor really well. All that together made him irresistible. At least to her.

- Why did you stink yourself that much? – Monika wrinkled her nose as if she were just cleaning her toilet bowl.

- Good morning to you too – Viktor laughed and kissed Nora on the forehead.

- It's a good thing you arrived just now, if you had come a second earlier, you would have witnessed a Shakespearean-like drama.

Viktor worriedly glanced at Nora.

- She's exaggerating – Nora grinned at him. She was feeling a lot better now and just wanted for this circus to be over.

- Let's go then, I parked in front of the building.

All three of them got into the car and arrived at the faculty building relatively quickly as it was late June, and the city got a little bit less crowded. Everyone rushed to take advantage of the first rise in temperature and the start of the seaside season. There was not any fuss or noise even at the faculty. Everyone was already on holiday. Nora, Viktor, and Monika walked into the building, and Nora thanked God that it was an old building with massive walls because inside, it was cold as if it was not the beginning of summer and scorching heat. She certainly would not like to start dripping with sweat in from of the professors who were paying close attention to everything she was saying and doing. She took Viktor and Monika to a small classroom on the second floor, where they were welcomed by two older male professors and a younger female professor. After a brief conversation, Nora completely relaxed and began presenting her thesis. Viktor and Monika were, as her guests, sitting in the back of the classroom and listened in fascination while Nora was effortlessly wielding all the technical terms and concepts. She was standing in front of the professors, holding only a laser pointer that she used to point out the important facts. While presenting her work, she was successfully engaging professors in the discussion, and visibly enjoyed the moment. She was born to teach; as soon as she started, there were no more jitters at all. The slide-show was cheerful and vibrant in color, forcing you to keep your eyes on it and pay attention. The presentation lasted for about half an hour, after which professors unanimously and very quickly decided on her final grade. After congratulations and enthusiastic praise from the professors, the three of them went to a luncheon.

- You killed it! – Monika shouted – Well done!

- Yes! We were mesmerized. Congratulations! – Viktor hugged and kissed her. Both of them surprised Nora with enormous flower bouquets, and she could not figure out where they hid them up to that point. She was beaming with joy and pride. All her studying was for this moment. She just achieved what she had been sacrificing and living for the last five years. The feeling was wonderful and irreplaceable.

- Thank you, thank you. The flowers are beautiful! Let's eat something because I'm starving!

They arrived at a restaurant and went all out with ordering food. The table was packed with soup, meat and side dishes, salads, and desserts. They sat there for a couple of hours, feeling like they would explode from overeating and drinking. But they did not care; it was time to celebrate. Nora was happy that the two of them were there with her. She knew they were genuinely happy for her accomplishments. They were her closest people in this far-flung city, but she still missed her mom and dad. But they would be here for her graduation, and then her success would be absolute.

*

The graduation was in early September. It was a big and significant ceremony for every graduate. Everybody brought their loved ones as guests and strutted around in their long graduation gowns and caps. Tassels on their caps that the graduates were supposed to move from the left to the right side during the graduation procession, demonstrating that they were now recognized members of the academic community, danced around as they walked. Nora's mom and dad arrived that morning, both as formally dressed up as the parents could be. They were both bursting with pride and smiled at each and every passerby as if all of them knew that their only daughter was becoming the queen of the universe that day. Because in their eyes, she had achieved nothing less than just that.

This was a special day; besides her graduation, Nora's parents would meet Viktor for the first time. It seemed like he was as nervous as she had been before her thesis defense. The only difference was that he had those jitters for the last two weeks. Nora was on the receiving end of his constant anxiety — how should he cut his hair, how should he shave, what should he wear to look formal, modest, manly, and worthy of their daughter — as he put it. Seriously? Has anyone ever described a garment like that? Viktor had simply lost his mind in the last few days, and she really hoped he would not make a total fool of himself while trying to make her parents like him. The plan was that she would spend the morning with them. They walked around Osijek, had breakfast, and went for a coffee. They laughed and talked like they used to when she was a little girl. She could see how much they had missed her and longed for spending some time with her. Dad held her hand the whole time, commending her success and saying how proud he was. Mom, however, kept kissing her, all emotional about her little girl who was not so little anymore. They were so sweet that Nora was on the verge of tears of all the happiness and overwhelming love they radiated.

Now they were sitting and waiting for Viktor. Nora looked at her parents and tried to see them the way he, a complete stranger, would see them. Dad seemed serious and dangerous at first, but in fact, mom was the one you should fear. She just looked timid, being tinier than dad, with a light auburn hair and deep dark eyes. Even her features were soft and warm. However, if she decided to put you in your place, you would work up quite a sweat before she was done

with you. She was determined and knew exactly what she wanted, persuasive and direct, holding all the strings, and in total control of everything. She was hard to fool, and if you got on her wrong side, you were doomed. On the other hand, dad was tall and robust, a manual worker. He was balding, so he shaved the rest of his head. He wore black-rimmed glasses and had mustache and beard, which made him look like a neighborhood badass, but actually, he was as loveable and sweet as a kitten. He would often calm his wife down and try to tame her temper while practically never losing his own. He was particularly sensitive about his only daughter, who could ask anything from him, and he would always please her. Nora could not wait for them to meet Viktor and to hear how they felt about him. As soon as she thought of him, she saw him making small, nervous steps towards them. He wore suit pants and a plain white shirt, ditching a tie so he would not look pompous, as he said.

The introduction went well if you asked Nora. However, for some reason, her dad, the most considerate and understanding person Nora knew, was not exactly impressed with Viktor. He just did not click with him, as he was quiet and glum the whole time; mom was nudging him under the table, but it did not help. Mom, on the other hand, accepted Viktor wholeheartedly – the two of them were toasting and joking around. It is interesting how things work out sometimes.

Graduation lasted about two hours. The students were called out, given their diploma and a rose, the professors congratulated them, and then they would stand in front of the audience and move their cap tassel from left to right to indicate that they had now concluded their five-year journey at this college. After that, the speeches were held and the caps were thrown into the air, which also marked the end of the graduation ceremony. Soon after, Nora, her parents, and Viktor proceeded to a restaurant, where they continued to celebrate. Nora was swamped with flower bouquets, and she was posing with her cap for a bunch of photos with everyone. Proud dad did not hide his admiration for his only daughter, but his disapproval of her choice of a man was equally obvious.

- Dad, come on, what's bothering you? – Nora hugged him as they walked to the apartment. Viktor left so she could have more time with her parents before they had to go home as well.

- Seriously, Stjepan, you're acting like a pigeon scared shitless! – mom was full of understanding.

- Nothing, what? I'm just feeling a little bit spaced out.

- You don't like Viktor – Nora looked him in the eyes.

- If I must confess, no.

At least he's honest, Nora thought.

- But why, he's a great guy – mom came to Viktor's defense.

- I just don't. It's something about him. I don't know what, but, well, I have the right to dislike someone – he shook his head and shrugged as if he were a child who wanted something, but could not explain what.

- Stjepan, I don't think you would like anybody because nobody would be good enough for your only child. It is what it is, whether you admit it or not – mom was shaking her hand as if she was shooing off the flies around dad's head.

- It's not like that. I simply...

She cut him off mid-sentence.

- You forgot what it's like to be a son-in-law and what it's like to want to be liked by someone. Not too long ago, you were in the same boat, remember? You have to give him a chance, this was a very brief encounter.

- Well, I never said that he was banned from being around me, only that I'm not so pleased now that I've met him – he glanced at Nora with a look of pure guilt.

- But, dad, he is so kind, and I really have a lovely time with him.

- Are you happy? – he paused and looked at her.

- Yes. If I weren't, I wouldn't be with him.

- If so, that's enough for me! We will deal with everything else – he smiled and hugged his daughter, kissing her on the forehead.

- That's right! And if I stop being happy, you'll be the first to know.

- And the first one to help you! Remember that – he said, all emotional.

- Oh my, let's hurry up to pack and go home before we all get mushy up in here – mom Marija was always the level-headed one. They just arrived at their car parked outside the building.

- Besides, you need to store all the preserves I brought for you in the pantry. Look, here is the cooked tomato, and some jam. All the bottles are labeled; you have the strawberry and apricot one. Beets and cucumbers are in these little ones, so you can eat it all at once when you open them. I brought you potatoes, French beans, and kidney beans. Everything is fresh, and it will last you for a long time. Let me help you. Also, I made you some homemade noodles, I know you like those. And breadcrumbs, for frying – mom started unpacking the bags full of food in the middle of the street. All that Nora could do was helplessly shake her head. Her mom always thought Nora would starve to death if she did not personally take care of her weekly menu. They struggled to drag it all up to the kitchen, and all of it barely fit the table and kitchen elements. Everything was clogged. Mom even took the unpacking into her own hands. She put in the fridge everything that needed to go there, and all the other food into the kitchen cupboards.

- And what are you planning now, sweetie? Are you going to look for a job here or in Kutina? – dad watched mom work. Nora knew what he wanted to hear, but that was not the answer she could give him.

- I'm staying here, dad. I'll look for a job here. I can work on a student contract for another three months, that's how I will get by for starters. And then I hope some jobs will come up.

He just nodded.

- Whatever you want. Dad and I support you in everything – mom interjected, even though dad seemed like he was on the verge of tears. Nora hugged him. She knew how hard it was for him. But she also knew she had to build her own path and happiness. After all, he also had to leave his parents, and so would Nora's children someday. That was the natural cycle, and it was entirely normal.

5

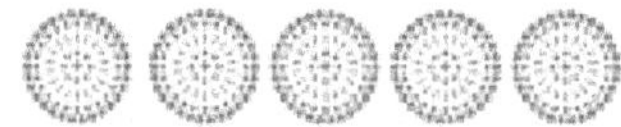

She was sitting on a barstool and leafed through the newspaper, and on every page popped up the breaking story of the trail of Ivo Sanader.[22] For a month, stories about the start of the trial of the former Prime Minister had been circulating all over the media. She shook her head because it was already coming out of her ears. The coffee bar was relatively empty that day. There were two couples outside on the terrace, but nobody was inside. Given that the guests were usually mostly students, who currently did not have classes, she was not surprised that there were no people. She drank her coffee with milk, while the fresh one was waiting for Viktor. Every day before work, he would stop by to kiss her and have coffee with her. He worked for his dad; they had a company that dealt with the maintenance of agricultural machinery. As they were their own bosses, Viktor had flexible working hours. So, for example, he would work from 9 AM so he would not be too tired. As if the rest of the world did not work from 6 or 7 AM. *The only-children are totally spoiled,* Nora thought. She opened up a horoscope page in the newspaper. She would never miss that one.

22   Translator's note: Former Prime Minister of Croatia (2003-2009) involved in a corruption scandal in late 2010 and sentenced to 10 years in prison on corruption charges in 2012

- I haven't slept all night! – Viktor stormed into the bar like a whirlwind.

- Good morning to you too – she smiled, raising her head to kiss him. But he walked right past her as if he did not see her. He was all breathless and flustered.

- My right groin has been hurting all night. I strained it playing football yesterday, and now the pain is not going away. I was reading on the internet about the possible consequences of muscle rupture. I'm in a complete state of shock. I could go lame on that leg or end up having a surgery! – he sat on the chair, all pale and visibly upset. Nora had to bite her tongue to stop herself from making a sarcastic remark. A person with a severe injury would not run around a coffee bar like a headless chicken, but that was just her lay opinion.

- I'm sure you just overdid it. As soon as you rest, it will get better – she handed him his coffee and a glass of water.

- I will not drink anything except water, I made an appointment to see my doctor, and she will see me right now because I told her it was urgent.

Nora stared at him with her mouth open.

- Oh, *okay*. And you won't drink coffee or eat anything because…? – he looked at her as if she said something stupidest in the world.

- Well, maybe they will have to take my blood.

Nora just shook her head in disbelief.

- Of course, yes… *The only checkup you need is the one with a shrink*, she thought. She got up and started washing her hands to distract herself from laughing. She would give anything to go to the doctor with Viktor and see him, after the leg and muscle checkup, sitting there and asking the doctor about a blood test. When she thought about it like that, the doctor really could send him to get tested. His head, though.

- I'll let you know how it went so you're not worried – Viktor kissed her hair. *Maybe the poor guy is so afraid, he didn't realize he was kissing the wrong side of my head?*

- Yes, yes! Be sure to, as soon as you know anything, sweetie – she yelled after him as he walked out. Only then she let herself laugh out loud. *God, I'm dating a lunatic.*

After the morning rush, which usually started around 9 AM, she took a moment to rest and get some air. She looked at the fountain in front of the bar, which looked like three completely open umbrellas on three levels from which the water was falling. For some strange reason, the sound of the fountain and the continuous pouring of water relaxed her. Monika used to laugh at her because of that, but that was clearly because she did not understand art at that level. Monika laughed at that explanation as well. Nora's phone rang as she was wiping down the tables. It has been about two hours since Viktor rushed to see the doctor.

- Hello, love? How are you? What did she say?

She wanted to ask a few more questions, like – *have you had the surgery yet*, but she assumed he might get offended at that much sarcasm.

- Imagine this! She said that there was nothing wrong with me and that I was taking up real patients' place. Well, I mean, everybody would get worried, right? You never know what could go wrong. I believe in that saying – better safe than sorry. But she was so rude that I'm thinking about changing my doctor. *And going to get a second opinion?* – it was right on the tip of Nora's tongue, but she refrained.

- Ah, my love. She's agitated because she's swamped. The important thing is that you are okay…

- Well, I feel a little bit better, but then again, it hurts.

- You need to rest. I'll come to your place tonight, and we'll watch a movie…

- Yeah, all right. And if I will have any problems with anything, you'll be there to help me – he said so sadly that Nora could not even roll her eyes at him.

Her shift was coming to an end as she was discussing job vacancies with Monika, which both of them had been closely following. It was already August, and the heat was hellish. She turned the air conditioner on high, even though it was already 8 PM. Both of them were excited about looking for a job, but no schools had issued any vacancy notices yet, because of the holidays, which made them terribly nervous. Monika worked a night shift that night. They worked in the same coffee bar, which was also a night club on weekends. When she handed the shift off to Monika, Nora went to the store to get some snacks, chocolate, fruits, and cold juice for her patient. He was waiting for her lying on the bed with his leg raised on three pillows. One would think that the leg was ready for amputation, no less. In his small kitchen, where every bit of space was used up in the best way possible, Nora found bowls and filled them with grapes and watermelon. She sat back next to him after she opened all the windows to get at least a gust of wind in. She fell asleep beside him, calm and peaceful. True, he was a weirdo, but he was her weirdo. He was the person with whom she spent her days and whose company she truly enjoyed. Before she realized it, those three months that she could still work on her student contract had passed. But her boss decided to keep her in the coffee bar, so she continued doing the same job, only on a different contract.

*

She could not stand Thursdays. She grumpily flipped through her calendar, counting the days until Christmas and thinking about how much longer she had to work in this wretched bar until some school bothered to issue a vacancy and, on top of that, hire her. She was annoyed at costumers, coworkers, annoyed at her boss, and all of the coffee machines. She was also irritable because she was supposed to start her period. Her breasts ached, and her ovaries wanted to fall out.

- Well, I'll explode until I get it – Nora complained to Monika. They worked this shift together.

- Haven't you got it yet?

- Well, no, I'm due these days – she waved to an older woman to let her know she saw her, the one that every day at the same time ordered coffee with Ledo[23] whipped cream and Pago[24] grape juice. As if programmed.

- I mean, I know we start periods about the same time, and I got mine ten days ago…

Immediately, Nora broke out in a cold sweat.

- When you say it like that, I don't actually know the exact day I'm supposed to get it. I mean, I have all the symptoms, just waiting for the period to start – she hurried to her purse to get a small calendar from her wallet, on which she was writing down her cycles. She counted three times until she was sure.

- Monika, for heaven's sake! I'm eight days late! – she frantically calculated days on the calculator, in case her panicky brain had problems with basic arithmetic operations.

- Are you sure? – her friend looked as terrified as she was.

- Yes! But how is that possible, I've been feeling pain every day. The same pain I feel before every period. Maybe I got a cold?

- Perhaps, yes, or stress. You've been stressing over finding a job – Monika tried to provide her with the last shred of hope.

- Oh, God, I'm pregnant!

- Oh, come on, don't get all dramatic! You just figured that out,

---

23   The largest Croatian manufacturer of industrial ice cream and the largest distributor of frozen foods

24   Fruit juice producer operating internationally, one of the most popular brands in Croatia

like, at this very moment? You will do the test first, and then you can make conclusions – Monika went to serve the woman who waved at them for the third time. Nora felt like running over to her table and stuffing that Ledo whipped cream into her head. Her mind was running a million miles per hour, and her hands started to shake. *Jesus freaking Christ, I'm pregnant. But how? I was supposed to start my period every day now, I'm sure these are menstrual symptoms.* She grabbed her breasts and squeezed them. She noticed some guy looking at her strangely so she turned away from the bar. *Well, they hurt me like crazy, I will get it any second now, I can't be pregnant. Yes, that's right. Although I was nauseous two days ago, and today, but that could be from anything.* After all, she had been feeling nauseous before getting her menstruation a lot of times.

- Well, I'm not pregnant – she announced to Monika when she returned. Monika looked questioningly at Nora as she was opening a beer and juice for an elderly couple.

- For real! I have to get my period, but it's still not alarming. If I don't get it until the end of this week, I'll take the test. But I can't be pregnant.

- I agree. After all, I told you exactly that. If you're going to stress about it like this, you're not going to get it anyway. Relax.

Of course, she had a mild nervous breakdown sixteen more times, and of course, she made Monika buy her a pregnancy test that same day on their way home because she was embarrassed to do it, and everyone would look at her and know what she was doing. As if someone actually cared what one Nora Pomat was buying in the pharmacy. And of course, she was biting her nails like crazy in their living room as Monika tried to figure out the test instructions.

- This definitely shouldn't be this complicated! I mean, it's not like you have to finish college to know, excuse my words, how to piss on a piece of plastic! It's their complicated instructions – Monika grumbled because the two of them were still sitting with an unopened test, after ten minutes, trying to figure out the instructions. Neither of them had ever taken the pregnancy test before, so this was a real challenge for them.

- All right, we got it! – Nora clapped her hands. She was panicking, but she was also eagerly waiting to be done with it.

- It'll turn out negative anyway – she concluded.

- It has to. There's no way it won't.

She peed into a cup, and Monika put the test in it right away.

- It says we should wait for ten minutes and then look. If two lines appear, it means you're pregnant. If there is only one line, you're not.

Nora stared at it as if she was trying to prevent the second line from forming by sheer willpower.

- What did you say the two lines mean? – her voice became squeaky.

- Two lines are an indication that you are pregnant, but wait ten minutes; you can't see it right away.

- But I can see it! I see two lines!

Monika ran to the table where that cup stood as a strange trophy.

- Impossible, it hasn't been even a minute.

- Does it say anything about the lines showing up before those ten minutes have passed? Maybe we didn't do it correctly? – Nora hopefully offered a solution.

- No… It doesn't say anything. Maybe that's implied?

Monika leafed through those little instructions of use in all directions as if she eas holding a thousand-page encyclopedia. Nora sat on the couch and stared at the test in the cup. Monika hugged her compassionately.

- Maybe that second line will disappear in ten minutes.

Nora laughed in desperation.

- God, Monika, I'm pregnant!

They looked at each other silently. Of course, it was a Thursday; everything terrible always happened to her on a Thursday. She really despised Thursdays. But for real!

*

Nora lay in bed and did not want to leave – ever. Fortunately, they had a day off that day. She was not able to fall asleep until dawn. Monika kept her company the entire night. They agreed to make an appointment for an urgent gynecological visit. Then they would probably know more. All night long, they had been reading online forums. They found out, still not with too much hope, that for a lot of girls who had their tests turn out positive, that was not the case in the end. Nora was worried about a million things. She did not have a job; she was not sure Viktor would be glad about all of this, they never actually talked about this kind of situation. In fact, Nora felt very foolish; she was dating this person, sleeping, and spending her time with him for a year and a half without even discussing the important life stuff. When she thought about it like that, she was sure he would not want this to happen; otherwise, he would have already raised such a topic. Her stomach turned in panic. What would her mom and dad say? She was not a child, but she was not entirely independent either – they still helped her financially, she worked in a local coffee bar for minimum wage, and she was desperately waiting to get a real job. This was definitely not according to her plan. It was supposed to go in this order – first, get a job and do the traineeship. Then pass the state exam. Marry and have three hundred guests. Have the biggest white dress ever. Have a carriage. Have all of her high school girlfriends as bridesmaids. Have a gigantic cake with two pigeons kissing. Later, get pregnant and be admired by everyone. Everybody would hardly wait to meet that baby. She would have her baby shower. And no one would comment on her being unmarried and pregnant. Or that the baby did not have a dad, or that the baby's dad only married her because of the pregnancy. By now, she was weeping. She felt so miserable and alone that she did not know what to do. She knew that she could count on Monika, but it was something she would have to go through on her own and had to deal with on her own. In a moment of panic, even abortion crossed her mind. That would be the easiest option; no one would know. But as soon as she thought of that, she scolded herself. She always had a clear stand about that. She was sure she could not do it. She took several deep breaths and went to take a shower to clear her mind. Monika was waiting for her with coffee on their small terrace. It was a meter by meter terrace. They barely crammed two small chairs and a coffee table, but they managed to bring it to life with a bunch of colors. They had decorative pink floral cushions, a green tablecloth, and two hanging plant pots with lots of pink-purple geraniums in them. Decorative string lights were hanging on the wall and gave off unique charm at night, as well as several pink and green lanterns with tealights in them. It was their small oasis of relaxation and peace. As the terrace was facing north, it was in the shadow of the nearby buildings almost constantly, so they spent most of their time there, especially on these hot summer days.

- I called a few practices. I managed to get us into one. They will have a free slot around noon, so we have to come, sit and wait. And pay, of course – Monika was really considerate, making Nora coffee and slicing some salami and cheese for breakfast. Nora barely ate anything; her stomach was all knotted up. How was she supposed to wait that long?

The practice was in a private building, on the third floor. The girls entered through the door and immediately saw that it was a private apartment that someone had adapted for this purpose. The doctor worked alone. He was an older man with glasses, with a pleasant voice and appearance. He was wearing white scrubs and told them to sit and wait until he was done with another patient. They sat in a small "waiting room" – if you could call it that way. It was obviously just a hallway with chairs and two flower pots. To the left was a door that led to his office, to the right was another door. Opposite them was a large window overlooking the children's playground, and next to it was a toilet. Nora would give everything in the world for the doctor to tell her that she was not pregnant; it would be the happiest day of her life. He invited her inside, and as she stripped down behind the screen, she felt sick and could not think about anything. She lay on the examination table, holding her breath.

- So, you think you're pregnant? Let's take a look — the doctor was really kind and friendly. He remained silent as he prepared the ultrasound. He repositioned himself and began the examination. Nora stared along with him at that black screen with occasional whitish shades. She was desperate to see what he saw in that, as she had no idea what was going on. One moment she was looking at him, another at the screen.

- Yeah… You see, this here is something I would undoubtedly suspect was a pregnancy. However, this is still small, and I can't confirm it with absolute certainty. But if the test turned out positive, I would definitely say it is a pregnancy. If you return in a week, we'll be absolutely sure — only then did he look at her and see her look of dismay. She seemed utterly hopeless.

- This is not the worst thing in the world, young lady. Don't be so shocked; we will talk about everything in a week — he smiled to reassure her. She made some kind of a grimace, hoping it would resemble somewhat to a smile, and hurried to pay him so she could go out to get some air.

Outside, still shocked, she drank the juice Monika had bought her. Her head was in chaos. *So that's it, I'm pregnant* - she said to herself, probably for the fiftieth time. Besides, she had to tell Viktor now. She was sick in her stomach, which threatened to bring back up all the five bites she had today. They were sitting in the fresh air, silent. Monika completely understood her, and she did not try to pull out some empty tales or try to comfort her with lame phrases; she was just there for her. When they arrived home, it was already late afternoon. Nora got ready to visit Viktor. It took her twice as long to get to his place than usual. The whole way there, she was trying to come up with a speech. She felt and looked like a dead man walking when she arrived in front of his building. She stared at his window for a moment, took a deep breath, and sighed. *Okay, this is it, what's the worst that can happen?*

Viktor was lying relaxed on the couch, watching a movie on the TV. As soon as she came in, he cheerfully waved at her, inviting her to come closer. He hugged and kissed her, so for a moment, she forgot about the burden she was carrying. He prepared dinner for them. It was a microwave pizza, though, but Nora appreciated the gesture nonetheless. The whole apartment smelled so nice that her stomach growled. No wonder, considering she had not eaten all day. She took a slice, then another, and eventually ate half a pizza in no time. She was still terribly nervous, but his presence calmed her significantly. She was waiting for the right moment to tell him, so she took advantage of the Coca-Cola advertisement when it popped up. She knew that, usually, commercials lasted longer than a movie bit between them, so she decided to tell him then. After this kind of conversation, it was improbable they would continue watching the movie, anyway.

- Sit down. I have something to tell you.

Alas! What a stupid way to start a conversation. Really? You've been thinking so much about what to say, only to come up with this?

He looked at her with a raised eyebrow and sat on a chair, his eyes fixed on her. She was even more uncomfortable now. She wanted to run. Maybe she still could. She could tell him she was just joking. Or that she missed him terribly. Or that they have not had sex in a long time.

Great, Nora, that kind of thinking got you in this situation in the first place. Stop being a fucking coward and spit it out.

- *Okay.* I'm pregnant.

Direct and to the point. Nora held her breath as she looked at Viktor's face, which was displaying a mixture of shock, understanding, and disapproval. Her heart sunk into her boots. He looked at her silently and rose from the table, strolling toward the door. *Wait, what? What the hell?* She stared at him. Before he grasped the door handle, he turned to her.

- Oh, fuck — he said so softly she had to strain her ears to hear it. He walked out.

6

Viktor walked around his hometown like he was in a dream. He did not notice which buildings or streets he was passing. Everything was a fog. Everything was far and unfamiliar. It was as if he was seeing the stadium, where he trained every day, for the first time. As if he had never passed by that bus station before. The bus station where he would wait for a bus every day in high school. As if he had never seen the bakery where he would drop by every morning to get meat burek. The people passing him by were just a moving blur of color he was noticing with the corner of his eye. His heart pounded deep in his throat, and there was buzzing in his ears. He struggled with every breath. Even though it was evening and the air was cooler, at least to some tolerable level, he still felt like he lacked oxygen and would pass out. He gulped in deep breaths and felt like a fish out of water. All of a sudden, even his legs did not listen to him; they carried him on their own and were getting shaky at the same time. He sat on a bench and propped his head with his hands. He did not know what to do with himself.

Pregnant? He was not ready for that; he had not even thought about it. There was no place in his mind for such a thought. Kids were a terrible hassle. He was not ready to dedicate his life to someone else. He had plans. He planned to work abroad, expand his business, emerge into the business world, and stand side by side with great employers. He wanted fame, money, and power. He wanted fancy lunches and gala dinners. He wanted sophisticated weekend getaways and powerful cars. He wished to share it all with his friends. Hell, he did not really want a baby at all.

He was watching some high school students playing basketball. Lucky them. Not a single worry on their mind. Certainly not even close compared to how he was feeling at that moment. *How did this happen? And why me? I should have been smarter. In fact, she should have been!* The enormous burden that fell on him made him feel rage towards Nora. *How can one woman allow herself to end up in this situation? Didn't she count those fertile days? Take care of some contraception?* Actually, how did they got to the point that he did not even know what protection they were using? Man, it obviously served them well until now. Maybe it was not absolutely confirmed yet? Then again, she would not have told him if she was not sure. She probably also did not like this situation. Maybe she wanted to have an abortion? For goodness sake, he did not even know what her stand on any of that was. It did not really matter; he should also have some say in it. What if he wanted her to have an abortion? She could not oppose him. He touched his forehead; he was feeling feverish as drops of sweat started running down his temples. The same thoughts kept going through his head again and again. And again. The panic did not ease up.

The next thought shook him to his core. What if Nora wanted this to happen? What if she did it on purpose? She is not getting any younger. Her girlfriends probably kept mentioning it. They all wanted to get married. Maybe she thought this was her last chance. She used him. And now she was laughing and gloating with them. How knew how many poor guys ended up like this. Damn women. Like spiders, they weave their nets around men. He shook his head; he needed to calm down. He got up and continued wandering the streets. His legs were still making his body follow. Annoyingly, he kept running into couples with strollers and small babies. Whenever he would see them, it seemed as if they had opened their mouths wide open, threatening to swallow him. He would rush to the other side of the street, hoping to run away from them. He reached his high school and entered the playground behind it. He sat on a tall well at the foot of an old oak tree. He did not know which was older, the well or the oak, but both had been there as long as the school, as some sort of a trademark. It was a gathering place during recesses, before afternoon matches, and nights out. Mostly for seniors. They earned it with their status, and the rest of the "kids" enviously watched them flaunting during recesses while fantasizing about the time that "honor" would befall them as well. He stared at the carved names on the oak. Three hearts. "Fran and Vanja" in one, "Ivan and Ivana" in the second, "Viktor and Tatijana" in the last, biggest heart. His brain rewound back to ten years ago. To the time he was a high school senior.

*

- Catch it! – Fran threw him a beer. The high school was nearing its end, as was the hot May. The principal could not deal with them any longer; everybody's minds were somewhere else, far from this school. They all felt awfully grown up and important. Viktor heard a familiar, pleasant sound of opening a beer can and took a few long, cold sips. He looked at his friend.

- Don't we usually start a little bit later?

- Yes, usually... But today we need it right from the morning – Ivan joined them, their third friend. They did not go anywhere without each other. They have been in the same class for twelve years. They played football together. They went out together. Together they were carousing around, and they were even planning a collective vacation that summer. They lived in a kind of symbiosis. Not a day went by without them seeing each other.

- What's up, old sport! – Ivan slapped Fran across his back and lay back next to them. They were lying at the foot of the oak tree, pushing their feet against the well.

- Where's my beer, comrade?

- I have told you a hundred times that I am not going answer to you calling me that. You just have to annoy me from the start, ha? I'm completely fucked up as it is.

- What is it? Vanja made you angry? – Viktor and Ivan grinned, provoking him.

- I wish… Something worse.

Ivan was grumpily murmuring and playing with some twig, drawing different shapes in the dust.

- Come on, spill it out, you're acting like a woman! Do we have to use force to get it out of you? – Ivan had a really short fuse. Viktor laughed so hard his beer came out of his nose; he was coughing for ten minutes before coming around.

- Vanja thinks she's pregnant.

Silence.

- What you say?

Ivan's jaw dropped to the floor. Viktor stopped his beer can halfway to his mouth.

- Pregnant? – Viktor repeated, in case he heard it wrong. Fran just nodded and kept staring at the dust.

- Oh boy, comrade…

Ivan rested his head on the oak and closed his eyes. Neither knew what to say to their friend.

- What now? – Viktor was glancing from one to another.

- Nothing. I don't know. I'm screwed, you guys. I don't know.

What should I do? I don't have any money. If I tell my dad, he'll kill me, you know how he is.

They nodded and looked at each other. One time, Fran's old man beat the crap out of him just because a neighbor complained that Fran had crossed to his side of the lawn with a lawnmower. Fran had looked like a freak for days, first all red and bloody, then purple and blue. The way it usually goes. They even suspected that he had broken his rib. Viktor never hated anyone as that old abuser and drunkard. Fran's mom died when he was little, so he was stuck with that scumbag. That was also one of the reasons he was spending all his time with Viktor or Ivan. There was no way he would mention this to his old man. They will have to find the solution on their own.

- Oh, man. Should we collect the money for abortion? I will ask some from my old man, I will tell him I need it for football boots — Viktor looked at Ivan, signaling him to offer something as well.

- She won't do it. She doesn't want to hear about it. She wants the baby. She's afraid of abortion.

- Will you marry her?

- I don't know, guys. I don't know anything. What should I do about her? She was supposed to go to college. I was planning to be nobody, anyway. But she was supposed to become somebody. You know how smart she is.

- Yeah, shit. We should get drunk tonight, relax you a little bit. Come to my place tonight, we'll go to the park — they got up quickly, as the school bell rang for the end of recess. They sat silently at their desks, each in their own thoughts.

Viktor rested his head on his hands and looked out the window at the treetops swaying in the wind. All that he could think about was how his friend had ruined his own life. Man. None of them wanted or even thought about having a baby. None of them was up to it or capable of anything like that. His plans, his future, were ruined.

Honestly, Viktor felt sorry for him. On their way home, they kept silently kicking the stones on the road. Neither of them wanted to interrupt others in their thoughts. They were all in the same mood.

- You know, this might not be the end of the world – Ivan kicked a stone into somebody's backyard.

- How could it not be? – Viktor interrupted even before Fran got a chance to speak.

- Well. You've been together for a long time. Certainly not the first ones that this has happened to. Both of you have finished school. You will find a job.

- That's what I was thinking, too; I'm not going to walk out on her for sure.

Viktor looked at his friend. He had never looked sullener or more serious.

- But then again, everything we have planned will be ruined… - Ivan punched him in the shoulder, making him stop himself half-sentence.

- What the hell is wrong with you? – he whispered to him. – Shut the fuck up!

- I know, but again, I've been thinking. I've been planning on marrying her anyway. And can you imagine, we created a little human, together. As much as I am scared, I'm also in awe. If you get me.

They smoked a cigarette, reached the bridge, and went their separate ways.

Viktor had been thinking about Fran's situation for a week, and as much as he tried, he saw nothing positive there. He thought his friend was just feeling sorry for himself, while Viktor wanted for the situation to be dealt with. He refused to accept that the three of them would no longer be a team, and would instead add some woman and a child to the mix. They all were a group of friends, far from it. Both he and Ivan had girlfriends; the three girls were also good friends.

They hung out with each other and spent time together. But he had always looked at it as a passing adventure. He could not believe that Fran would really stay with her. That he would close himself into a house like the old married couples did; that he would take care of her and the baby, that he would work. Viktor would never allow such a thing to happen to him. He was grossed out even thinking about it. If Tatijana got pregnant, he would not stay with her. He was too young, and his whole life was ahead of him. He just was not that type. Neither would he ever be.

- Guys, false alarm! – Fran flew into the garage, where Viktor and Ivan were repairing some old motorcycle.

- She's not pregnant! She was late because of some inflammation – Fran was as happy as a sandboy.

- Well, congratulations, comrade! – Ivan slapped him on the back.

- Way to go, you dodged a bullet! – Viktor wholeheartedly smiled.

- Yeah, but it would've been interesting to see what'd happen… – Fran sat back on the couch and put his feet up on the table. It was Viktor's grandfather's old garage. Now, it was behind the main barn where his father kept large repair machines. They worshiped that garage; it was their space, and no one ever bothered them there.

- I'm telling you, you're better off this way. I would never be ready for something like that. Awful.

Viktor threw himself next to him, and Fran looked at him.

- Maybe not for Tatijana, but for someone you really care about… Trust me. It is scary, but somehow you calm down soon enough. And I calmed down so much that I almost wish it was true – he grinned.

- Just imagine me getting a son. One just like me. Well, hey, I would be the king of the world! – the other two burst into laughter.

- Look at him, he's already getting all mushy about the baby.

- I don't know what is funny about all of that, guys. To me, it's like my worst nightmare – Viktor ended the discussion, and each of them focused on doing their part in trying to get that motorcycle up and running again after a very long time.

*

He flinched at the sound of a motorcycle. He was still sitting alone at the old well. Only now he was in his own worst nightmare. Now there was no Fran that Viktor could feel sorry for; now, he only felt sorry for himself.

7

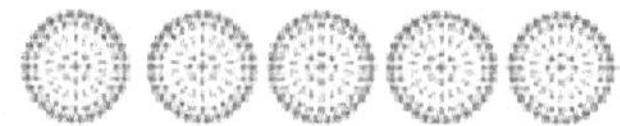

Nora was walking around the apartment like a caged lion. He did the worst thing he could! He could have yelled, sworn, cried – everything would be more reasonable than this! *Who does that? Who gets silent and disappears after hearing news like that?* Nora was furious. So much so that she knocked over all of his football trophies, which he had lined up on an improvised dresser mounted to a wall. She wanted to scream. She kept looking through the window every thirty seconds to see if he was coming back; he had been gone for four hours. He did not even take his cell phone.

She had no idea where he was or what was in his head. As far as she knew, he might have killed himself. She scolded herself. She could not think like that. It was crazy to think that he would find the thought of them building a life together so revolting that it would make him take such a drastic measure, right? She burst into hysterical laughter. Monika called her several times, each time listening patiently to Nora's nervous breakdowns, which had now reached double digits. She had to leave. He may be lurking in the bushes somewhere, waiting for her to get bored of waiting and leave his apartment. After all, if he did not want to deal with her, he had to wait for her to go away. Maybe that was the reason he was gone. Nora found her backpack and, with shaky hands, began packing the things she had left in Viktor's apartment. She was not going to force him into anything. She would figure something out, she was humiliated enough. She was reaching for her old pajamas, which were pushed to the highest shelf when she heard the door open. She stood motionless in the bedroom, listening – did she really hear that or did she imagine the sound out of pure desire for those damn door to finally open.

- Nora?

Familiar deep voice. He came back. After four hours of hell, Viktor came in and was calling out her name as if it was just an ordinary day. She walked into the living room, her hands shaking even harder. He stood there with a grocery bag.

- I brought us something to eat.

- I'm not hungry – she barely uttered. She wanted to physically attack him. *Who cares about the food right now! Tell me what's in that head of yours. Why were you gone for so long? Say everything you have to say so we can get end this awful suspense!* Out of all that she could possibly say, she just mumbled that she was not hungry.

- I'm sorry I just left like that. I needed to be alone to process my thoughts.

She nodded, at least he was smart enough to apologize.

- I've been going out of my mind. I felt terrible.

- I know, I'm sorry. I really am.

He approached her and held her hands.

- When are you working next week?

- What?

She was more than confused. Why the hell was he asking her that right now? Why was it important?

- When are you free so we can move you?

She was staring at him, trying to process his words. Only able to stand there, paralyzed while uncontrollably blinking. He smiled.

- Don't be so shocked at the prospect of living with me.

She did not get it wrong. Viktor was really offering her to come live with him.

- You're asking me to move in with you?

He nodded.

- You could've said that right away, not leave me in this apartment to contemplate for four hours what should I break next. We wouldn't be left with any furniture if I wasn't as cool-headed as I am — she gasped, tears running down her face. He would not leave her alone. They would get through it together, and everything would be alright.

- Well, as far as I can see, my trophies weren't that lucky. They made your cool-headedness yield, I guess — he grinned and put their dinner on the table.

*

Nora was packing the last box. Monika was handing her books, which they then carefully wrapped in newspapers as if they were made of porcelain. Two weeks have passed since the incident. In the meantime, the gynecologist confirmed the pregnancy with 100 percent certainty. Nora started having morning sickness, which she could barely handle. The doctor consoled her and said that, for most women, nausea stopped around fourteen weeks. She was eight weeks pregnant, which was barely halfway, and there was still hope that she was one of those women, even though she, deep down, doubted that. She was always the exception. Even her morning sickness did not come in the morning, like for most women; she was tortured by it day and night. Sometimes, it was so bad that she wanted to die.

They decided that Nora would move in with Viktor while they were having dinner on that fateful day. She would not say anything to her parents until it was all done. Such a simple solution, after all that stress eating them alive. Thinking about it now, she felt ridiculous. Why would she even believe that Viktor would walk out on her? He was a good man, she would not be with him if it was otherwise. After all, this was his child too.

- Don't forget your blanket. And, I'm begging you, take that abomination of a flower that looks like it's been dead for decades with you.

Monika was running around the apartment, not allowing Nora to lift anything heavier than a coffee cup.

- You don't want to keep it as something to remember me by? — Nora was teasing her.

- Remember you? You're moving ten minutes away from here. The moment I start missing you, I'll be at your door.

She jumped to her side and rubbed her belly.

- Or coming to rescue my godchild from the crazy parents.

Nora laughed heartily. As much as she was happy and excited about the start of a new chapter in her life, she was also nostalgic for her life with Monika. For years, they were everything to each other. They got used to each other, and it was not easy for Nora to just forget about it like that. Monika seemed to read her mind.

- There, there. Let's not mope around. You know who will be the happiest you're leaving? The cat, he'll finally have a room for himself.

They laughed. Nora wanted Monika to keep all the things that they had bought together, even though Monika insisted otherwise. But their apartment was a real dump without all those things, while Viktor's was newly furnished. Nora could do without them, regardless of the memories. She only took her pictures from the closet. They were glued on both doors. A bunch of photographs of people and moments dear to her.

- I think that's everything – Nora clapped her hands.

- I'll go through everything. And if you've forgotten something, it will be at your door in no time.

Viktor rang the bell to help them carry things.

- Here I am, my ladies. I'm ready to be the luggage handler.

- We've been waiting long enough.

Monika would probably never completely forgive him for those four hours of hell her pregnant friend had to go through because of him.

- I brought ice cream to redeem myself. Pregnant ladies are the first to choose.

That was a special night for both of them. Nora had slept over at Viktor's place many times before, but this was different. This time it was real. This time it was their place. Cluttered with boxes, but still, the place they were going to spend their time, where they were going to come with their baby and be a family. Long into the night, they just lay and talked about everything. Neither of them could fall asleep with excitement. They made a big step, and it felt so good. And if something feels that good, it must be right.

- I'm just going to go over to the firm to deal with something, you can slowly start getting ready. Mom said lunch was at 1 PM – Viktor kissed Nora's forehead. They arranged lunch with his mom and dad. Nora would meet them for the first time and immediately have to tell them she was pregnant. She was a little bit nervous since she knew that they were extremely traditional, so she did not know what kind of reaction to expect. Nora and Viktor called Nora's parents the day before and told them the happy news. They were overjoyed. Nora did not know who was more pleased, mom or dad. They did not overthink the fact that she was so young or that she did not have a job. They could not stop talking about their future grandchild and how they would do anything for that kid. They promised to provide a lot of support and help. For twenty minutes, her mom drowned Nora in advice on how to ease nausea and what to eat. Although she had known that they would be glad and not judge her, Nora was still surprised by their enthusiasm and happiness. She really did have the best parents in the world. Encouraged by their reaction, Nora felt a lot better about the lunch with Viktor's parents. She wore a light summer floral dress and bought flowers and coffee for his parents. They were both excited when they knocked on the door and were greeted by his mom Vesna. She was a well-dressed woman; you could tell she was taking good care of herself. Her hairstyle and makeup, as well as her outfit, suited her age and slim figure. She kept some distance from Nora, but also Viktor. His dad, Mate, on the other hand, was a gentle giant. Round and grey, red-faced, but loud and smiling. He hugged and kissed them both and led them to the table.

Their house was beautiful. Everything in it was brand new but decorated in a traditional style that Nora could not quite define. The living room was her favorite room because it had large windows that brought in so much daylight you had a feeling as if you were sitting in a backyard. A three and a two-seater sofa and a gray armchair with blue decorative pillows were all aimed towards a large TV screen. In the middle, there was a blue carpet and a small coffee table on it, with the remote controls and a fruit bowl neatly laid out. On the wall above the two-seater was a large wall clock that looked as if it belonged in a museum. It was the same shade of brown as the coffee table, with two large, intricately decorated hands making rounds on what, to Nora, looked like old yellow canvas. She observed it for so long that Mate turned to her mid-sentence and said that the clock belonged to his mother, who had brought it to the house as dowry. It has been in the family for years.

Lunch was sumptuous and delicious. Vesna paid attention to every detail. From serviettes to knife placement. Another character trait of hers, a perfectionist. *This one's going to be hard to impress*, Nora thought. After lunch, they sat down on the patio to have coffee.

- We came here to tell you that we are expecting a baby. Nora is pregnant.

Viktor did not think that beating around the bush would make it easier for anyone. Their expressions were priceless. Vesna looked as if she swallowed a teaspoon she had just used to stir her coffee. Only her eyes quadrupled, emphasizing her uptight and skinny frame. Mate clapped his hands like a little kid, and his face got even redder, if at all possible.

- You really took us by surprise, son. Congratulations!

Dad was the first one to talk. Although visibly surprised, he did not hide his joy. Vesna, however, still did not express any other emotion other than pure bewilderment.

- Mom, you won't say anything?

- Yeah… Well, this is quite a surprise. I mean, it's all so fast, we just met Nora, but great news, of course – she sputtered between two sips of coffee. Interesting woman.

- We feel the same way. But we are thrilled – Viktor took Nora's hand and smiled at her. That reassured her.

- But we should start planning the wedding immediately. It would be best if I contact a priest right now. We have a family friend, he will understand the situation and make the best of it.

Vesna got up from the table to get her cell phone.

- We haven't even thought about the wedding yet, mom.

- Excuse me? What will you do then?

- We wanted to take it slow, we haven't talked about it yet – Nora interjected.

- Sweetheart, you don't want to live in sin, do you?

Vesna looked at Nora like she was a moth mindlessly ramming into a lamp, which will inevitably scorch it.

- We just haven't decided yet, we have time. Now we have…

Vesna cut her off mid-sentence.

- There is nothing to decide. It's the way it should be. I don't even see the point of talking about it. I'll take care of everything.

She got up and disappeared into the house. Nora and Viktor sighed, and Mate poured them some šljivovica[25] to toast. Nora then realized why he was so red all the time. They spent the rest of the afternoon in a tense and uncomfortable atmosphere. Dad Mate kept refilling their glasses, while mom Vesna was getting more and more absent. Nora could hardly wait for them to leave. This afternoon would not make anyone's top five of the best family moments, she was sure.

The next day, she called her own parents to tell them about the meeting. Mom could not wait to hear what it was like. Poor thing probably spent the entire morning waiting next to her phone, so she would not miss the call.

- Have you mesmerized them? Who wouldn't be mesmerized by my stunning daughter? – she was chirping into the phone.

- I almost have – Nora laughed.

- What did they say?

- I think they are happy; they were quite surprised.

- Don't worry, when the baby comes, they will forget all about it. When they see those little eyes and legs, they will instantly fall in love.

The very mention of the baby got her mom all emotional.

---

25   A fruit brandy made from damson plums (plum brandy), produced in Central and Eastern Europe. In Balkan countries, it is considered a type of *rakija*.

- I hope so. We decided to get married.

Silence.

- You guys haven't mentioned that before.

- You're right, but his parents are very traditional, and we think it's for the best.

She was clearly on speaker because her dad interfered.

- Only if that is something that you want to do, kiddo. You don't have to do anything that doesn't feel right.

- I know, dad; I want to. I love Viktor, and I think it's the right decision.

- If so, my dear, you have our full support.

She ended the conversation and looked out the window.

Yes, I want to. It is for the best.

8

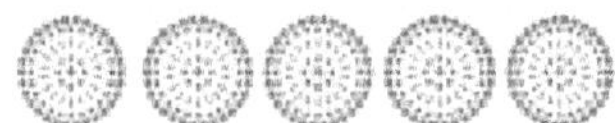

Nora woke up at 4 AM, that being the sixth time that night. Freaking peeing. She had to go to the toilet every half an hour. She was afraid to even think about what would happen further along in pregnancy. Her belly was barely visible, yet her bladder was on the verge of exploding. Viktor was sleeping like a log next to her. She wanted to shake him just so he could see what it was like not to be able to sleep. She was fourteen weeks along, and tomorrow, actually today, they were going to the gynecologist appointment. She was hoping they would get to find out the baby's sex. She was fed up with Viktor's aunts and neighbors having their gender-theories based on the way she scratched herself, the hand she was drinking with, the way she was getting out of a car, or opening a door. She found it astonishing that even today, these women believed in that nonsense.

Viktor woke up around 9 AM, just in time to discover Nora sitting and crying in front of the TV.

- What happened?

He jumped in panic in front of her, while she sobbed so hard that she could not put together a coherent sentence.

- Nora! What's wrong? – he shook her arms.

- This is so sad! Mom…does…not…let…him…marry…who…he wants… – she stuttered word by word between blowing her nose. It took Viktor a moment to realize she was talking about the movie she was watching. He had heard that pregnant women tend to have mood swings, but now that he had experienced it first hand, he did not know how to act. Women… Truly peculiar creatures.

- Honey, don't upset yourself, it's just a movie.

- But he's a prince. He should be with whoever his heart desires. And she loves him too. But now she left him after all.

He did not have a clue what she was talking about, nothing made sense. He opted for a different tactic.

- I'll make us breakfast, love. You take a shower and calm down, and then we'll go to the doctor.

Fortunately for him, the food did the trick every time. Weird combination, nonetheless, but who was he to judge a woman carrying another human being inside of her.

- You were right, I needed that.

When she returned from the bathroom fifteen minutes later, she was a different person. She was laughing and joking as if she had not just blown half a pack of tissues from crying.

- Just for you, boiled eggs and *ajvar*[26] – he presented a nicely prepared plate in front of her. She ate ajvar with a spoon. On its own.

Viktor was standing right next to her head as the doctor was pointing out tiny legs and arms, head, stomach, and the position of the baby on the screen. At first, Nora could not see whatever the doctor was showing them, but since Viktor was nodding so confidently, she

---

26   A condiment made from roasted or cooked red bell peppers and oil, used in the Balkans cuisine

did not want to seem stupid. But just hearing baby's heartbeat and seeing the baby move was enough for her. Viktor, however, was full of questions, so much so that Nora was sure the doctor would regret letting fathers attend these scans.

- I always save sex-reveal for last because that way, parents actually listen to what I have to say prior to that moment. If I reveal it too soon, they tend to not pay attention to anything else until the end of the scan.

Viktor and Nora stared at the screen with anticipation.

- What do you think it is?

- A girl – Viktor blurted out. Lately, he often expressed a wish for a little princess. Nora would freak out about it because if it was a boy, that would make it seem like they did not want him.

- I'd say that it is a… Little girl. Of course, we have to wait a little bit longer to be 100 percent sure, but this would suggest that it's not a boy – he laughed and congratulated them.

They spent the rest of the afternoon shopping for baby things. It was hard to resist little baby clothes, as they were checking out strollers and cribs. Their excitement was so palpable that Nora thought her heart would burst with happiness. Viktor chose several dresses with pink and purple tulle. Nora was cracking up while teasing him that his son would have to wear those if the doctor had made a mistake, to which he just sniffed at as if it did not concern him.

They did not spend a lot of time wedding planning. His parents, or rather his mom, insisted it was as soon as possible, while Nora's belly was still unnoticeable. Nora was not worried about that; they had decided to invite only their parents, a best man, and a maid of honor anyway, so she did not care if her belly was visible or not. All the closest people to her knew she was pregnant. Mom Vesna got very involved in the organization; she arranged a priest and a restaurant. Nora only managed to intervene in the food choices, at least somewhat, while

Vesna took charge of everything else. Both her mom and Monika asked Nora if she had not wanted a bigger wedding, with a real wedding dress and lots of people. Maybe she did a long time ago, but it was not so important anymore. At least that was what she told herself; this was the best way.

They were sitting in a restaurant, eight of them. Marija and Monika admired the view of the Drava river, while Stjepan observed the fireplace built into the wall. Surrounded by bricks, it gave a rustic note and the aura of luxury to the whole space. The soup was just served, and everyone was talking and laughing. Nora was wearing a long white dress, which looked more like an evening than a wedding dress, but she still looked really nice. Her dad had told her several times that she looked like a princess. The wedding ceremony did not take long, and she quite liked it. Their priest friend was exactly the way priests should be, kind and loving. He delivered a truly beautiful sermon while officiating the ceremony. They agreed the christening would be bigger and more formal, and that he would officiate again. After a festive lunch at the restaurant, which went quite long, Nora's mom and dad went with her and Viktor to their apartment, where they agreed to spend the night, instead of driving late to Kutina. Nora talked to her mom long into the night, sharing their pregnancy experiences and discussing childbirth. Mom caressed and kissed her belly hundreds of times. She described how she had felt when she found out about her pregnancy with Nora. It was a difficult birth, but Marija would have endured anything for her baby Nora. She was telling her how nothing in the world was so beautiful and as magnificent as the moment you get to hold that little baby, so vulnerable and entirely dependent on you. You just fall in love immediately. No one can replace it, and you forget about all the pain and agony. Nora listened to her blithely and absorbed her every word. You can only talk about those things with your mom. Nobody can replace your mom.

*

- I would never have guessed you would be the first one to marry –

Sofija had just finished her drink and was already signaling the waiter to bring her another one.

- Yeah, I agree. I never thought any of us would get married without the rest of us present – Nora sadly shook her head.

- It's interesting how life takes us its own course, whether we like it or not.

*

Viktor organized a honeymoon as a surprise. He booked them a trip to Istria.[27] A few days after the wedding, for that matter, but who's counting. He was so romantic and endearing it melted Nora's heart. They had three overnights in Rovinj, as well as the organized excursions to Pula and the surrounding towns. It was February and quite cold, but it was an enjoyable experience. She had never visited seaside cities in the winter; everything looked like a scene from a fairytale. Every day they went out to restaurants for lunch, and for walks or in bars in the afternoon. Viktor did his homework so he could take her to the best-rated restaurants in Istria. She enjoyed tastings and trying out new flavor combinations; she concluded that she definitely fell in love with truffles. They visited monuments and beaches. Nora wished they could stay there for longer because they were finally alone. Without his parents coming with unsolicited advice. Without him needing to leave for work. Without her panicking about job vacancies and why none of the schools were calling her back. It was just the two of them. Like in the beginning. Viktor could not thank her enough for agreeing to a smaller wedding and for accepting his parents as they were. He was well aware that his mother was a person who likes to impose herself, but he would find it really difficult if they had to go through any arguments or discussions. He and their baby were the only important thing to Nora now, their peace and happiness. She felt like they could go through anything together and that there was

---

27   The largest peninsula in the Adriatic Sea shared by Croatia, Slovenia, and Italy, but mostly encapsulated by Croatia

nothing in the world that could change that. They had each other, and that was enough.

If you asked Nora, she dealt with pregnancy pretty well. Viktor would agree, but only if she was listening. She had intriguing wishes that he would always grant, no questions asked, despite how strange and unrealistic they were. She managed to make him go on a hunt for salted pretzels without salt or out-of-season raspberries all over the city. He was always happy to do it, he had all the understanding in the world and wanted to help and make it easier for her any way he could.

She could not wait for the fruit season. She longed for cherries and strawberries, raspberries and blackberries, watermelon and melon so much throughout her pregnancy that there was a good chance of her daughter turning out to be some kind of a vegan. When the cherry season started, she was seven months pregnant, and her belly was getting huge. Once, she overate so much that she could barely breathe and was sure she had crushed the baby. For the next hour, she lay on the couch, trying to persuade her daughter to kick or move, purely to make sure she was okay. The stress about gaining too much weight was getting the best of her. Viktor found her roundness so adorable that he just had to continually hug and kiss her. He could feel his daughter kicking. He would sit for hours talking to the belly and caressing it, trying to feel the wobbling movements under his hand. It always seemed small and hard, so they loved to guess what body part it was. In the meantime, they had prepared a crib and purchased a stroller. His mom helped with washing and ironing baby clothes because Nora found it hard to deal with the heat this far in the pregnancy. She could not sleep at night, had trouble breathing, and a bad case of heartburn, as well as the pain in the abdomen that was stretching. Sometimes, her panic about childbirth or all that awaited them after the baby was born was getting intense. But the hours spent sitting and talking and singing to her belly made it all more bearable. She was simply fascinated by the miracle that was about to happen to her.

9

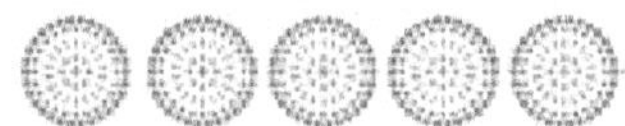

Everything was ready for another movie afternoon, and today was Nora's turn. In fact, if she thought about it, it had been her turn to pick a movie for the last six months. It was just one of those things Viktor has been doing that she did not even notice, but they were wondrous. She could feel a rush of hormones kicking in again, which only amplified the fact that, in that moment, she loved him more than ever. Just because he has been watching her dumb movies for six months straight.

- What are we watching? – he asked as if he did not know she had another sappy, romantic comedy or drama ready.

- *The Fault in Our Stars* – she answered, with a lump in her throat.

- Please don't tell me you're crying already.

- I read what it is about. Amazing movie.

- Here you go, then, amazing popcorn as well. We can start – Viktor said, sat next to her, and put her feet on his lap. He played the movie and began gently massaging her feet. He has been aware of his love for her for a long time. He would do anything in the world for her. He knew that she loved him just as much, and that was giving him a sense of security he had never felt before. The feeling when someone like her wants you for themselves. And on top of that, she was carrying his child. Nothing else had ever been as meaningful as that.

- Nora? The couch is wet. Did you need to go to the toilet?

- You consider me an idiot? Probably something spilled – she stood up and tried to figure out what happened. Suddenly she realized her leggings were wet too.

- Oh, my God, Viktor, I peed myself. I've had enough of this pregnancy, it turned me into a total fool.

She felt fluid going down her leg. She turned to go to the bathroom, but she did not get far. She felt something like a spasm in her stomach, only stronger than ever before. A few moments later, it happened again. She grabbed her stomach, and Viktor was already on his feet.

- Oh, it seems like your water broke.

It took their brains less than a second to realize what was happening, but it seemed like forever. Nora instinctively began taking deep breaths as if her body was preparing her for what was about to happen, and Viktor started running around the apartment. A hospital bag was ready next to the bedroom door. He grabbed that first. His keys were on the bar, and his phone on the balcony. Where was his wallet? In his jacket in the hallway. He was running from one side of the hall to another, trying to get everything they needed, while Nora stood by, breathing and convincing herself that this was really happening.

- Please, Viktor, take care of that water on the floor.

- I seriously don't think that's so important right now. Let's go. I have everything. Just take it easy – he took Nora's arm, holding her belly with his free hand.

Nora turned to him and gently kissed him on the mouth. She was trying to calm him down by showing him that she was okay and that everything would be okay.

- The doctor explained this part to us. We have a lot of time, so I'm going to take a quick shower and dress, and you pick up that water on the floor. We will go one step at a time – she said as if she was trying to calm both him and herself down. It took her about 15 minutes to shower and dress for the hospital. She was nervous, but from all the reading and research she had done, on top of continually harassing her doctor with questions, she was aware that this would take hours. They grabbed all the things that were ready to go and headed toward the car. Viktor helped her get in the passenger seat, tossed the bag in the back seat, and got behind the wheel. He was focused on the road like never before. Now it was Nora's turn to panic.

- Viktor?

- We are almost there.

- I really don't want to do this anymore. I'm scared. Please, let's go home.

- Honey, I don't think it works like that. Everything will be fine.

- You don't know that and don't say stupid things when you don't know. Okay?

- I know that part. Everything will be alright. For sure – he laid his hand on her stomach – I promise.

- Here it goes again – Nora clutched her belly and motioned to Viktor to time the contractions.

- 15 minutes.

Nora was scared, and he could tell.

Viktor turned on the radio. He would often use cheap tricks that he knew would always put a smile on Nora's face. If he could be sure of anything, it was his ability to make her laugh. While Nora was focused on breathing, Avicii's *Wake Me Up* started playing in the background.

\- How fitting – Nora said, and laughed.

That was it. Everything was okay when she laughed.

It took them seven minutes from Martin Divalt Street to the hospital. Viktor stopped at the entrance and quickly led Nora inside. He heard someone yell after him to move the car, so he answered that he would be right back. The nurse at the counter told them to sit down for a while and wait for her to call them in.

\- Are you kidding me right now? Which part of "she's giving birth" did you not understand?

\- I am not kidding. Sit down, and somebody will come to get her.

While Viktor was still perplexed by those instructions, Nora headed toward an empty chair. He helped her sit down, and soon after, another nurse arrived. She called Nora, and they made their way to the room. Viktor followed them, but the nurse told him he could not go any further. He only managed to kiss Nora and whisper to her that everything would be fine and that he was waiting right there. He looked after them as they disappeared further in the hallway, feeling the strangest mix of emotions ever – fear, excitement, concern, happiness, and helplessness, all at once. He heard that lovely person at the counter shouting and walked outside to move the car from the entrance.

Nora was led into the room and placed on a bed. She managed to not think about anything except her breathing. She concentrated so hard on that everyday act that she felt like it was the only thing keeping her together. The doctor examined her and said that everything was fine, but that she should be prepared for several hours of labor. Her cervix needed to be more open before they transfer her to a delivery room. They asked her if she wanted them to invite Viktor to be with her until then. Within minutes, Viktor stood by her side and held her hand.

Two hours had passed, and Viktor was still timing her contractions. Every time he thought a contraction hurt Nora more than the one before, he would go get a nurse.

- Nurse, could you come, please? – he called her in panic as soon as he saw her walking down the hallway.

- Of course – she said sarcastically, knowing what was up. Over the years, she had learned that fathers, especially first-time dads, had no capacity to remember information she had repeated at least 15 times.

- I think this is it. Contractions are 12 minutes apart – Nora said as the nurse approached her bed.

- Yes, and she also started to breathe weird – Viktor added.

- Aham, *okay*. Firstly, she is breathing heavy because she is in labor. It will only get harder – the nurse spoke to Viktor as calmly as she could, considering she had told him the exact same thing ten minutes ago.

- Mommy, you still have a long way to go. This part can last up to ten hours. I know it's hard and unfamiliar, but we are keeping an eye on you – she told Nora, hoping that it would make Nora forbid Viktor to call them every minute. It did not help.

Viktor tried to relax Nora by talking and making her laugh, but as time went by, she found it less and less entertaining. They had been in the labor room for five hours, and she just wanted to get some sleep. Contractions were getting closer together, and Viktor was calling the nurse even more often. The nurse explained that he had to calm down because they had several pregnant women who were much closer to giving birth and that they were keeping an eye on all of them, but that she was not able to stop by every five minutes. If she had any strength left, Nora would have told him to calm down and stop making the nurse angry because she needed as many of them on her side as possible. But she was scared too. All of this was new to her, and just like Viktor, every ten minutes she thought the baby was coming out and that the doctors were just not paying any attention.

After just over six hours of labor, at 9:13 PM the nurse called the doctor. He examined Nora and decided it was time for a delivery room. They sent Viktor to a waiting room, and Nora began preparing for giving birth. *This is it. This part counts, Nora,* she was saying to herself to lessen the fear she was starting to feel. They placed her on a table, as the contractions were getting stronger. Surrounded by strangers, afraid, and in pain, Nora could feel that she was losing her strength. The nurse guided her through the delivery, yelled at her, and made her push. Halfway through it, she wanted to tell them all to stop and that that was enough. If the baby did not want to come out, be it. Let her stay inside. She felt like she had used up every last drop of strength with each new push. But then, she would push again, every time. She had no sense of time because she did not know how the end of the birth looked like. The nurse laid the baby on Nora's chest. There were no words to describe that feeling. It was a lifelong bond. Unbreakable and more potent than anything else in the world. After four hours, at precisely 1:27 after midnight, a beautiful little creature that would soon change many lives came into this world.

*

Viktor spent all of those four hours pacing around the waiting room. He would try to sit down from time to time, but that would not last. The waiting room wall at Osijek Maternity Hospital was entirely written out. *Zid sreće,*[28] as they called it, had hundreds of names of children who had been born here written all over it. It witnessed one of every parent's strongest emotions. Viktor wondered where all those kids were now. What kind of people have they become or were about to become? What would his child be like? It is not so cool if you, as a parent, screw up a part of your child's upbringing that determines what kind of a person would your child turn out to

---

28   The Wall of Joy

be one day. He felt fear and excitement. He was worried about Nora and prayed that everything would turn out well. He was not even aware of doing it, but while he was staring at the names on the wall, he caught himself praying. A few minutes later, the nurse walked into the waiting room with the most beautiful little bundle he had ever seen. She told him that he could look at her for a moment before they had to take her back, and he felt a tear running down his cheek.

- How's my wife?

- Tired, but good. The girls were great.

He had to wait for a while, but he managed to persuade the hospital staff to briefly let him go to Nora's room. He approached her bed and gently kissed her forehead. She was tired and could barely keep her eyes open, but he had to tell her something before going home.

- Nora, I saw her. I've never seen anything so beautiful in my life. She looks just like you. I love you, and thank you for making me a dad – the tears stopped him from finishing. Nora pulled him in, and tenderly kissed him. She was happy and in love with her life. With her husband. With her beautiful child. She was in love with love.

Viktor stayed by her bed until she fell asleep and then went home. He let Nora's parents know that they had just become the grandparents of a beautiful little girl. Marija had never heard better news in her life. He also called his parents and told them he was on his way to their house. He called Monika, too. He called everyone he could think of, actually. This was the kind of news everyone must know. He became a dad!

He had parked in front of the entrance and heard loud music as soon as he got out of the car. He walked through the house into the backyard and saw his friends and parents gathered around the fire, roasting a whole suckling pig. They were drinking and dancing along to *tamburica*[29] players from the neighborhood. His mom was the first to hug and congratulate him. She was beside herself with joy, and for the first time in his life, Viktor saw his dad crying. It was his dad who, in just one hour, gathered everyone and organized everything to properly celebrate his granddaughter's arrival to the world.

According to an old custom, the Belajec family's backyard was decorated as soon as possible. Viktor's friends threw pieces of white cloth and feathers all over the yard, and he, according to tradition, had to treat them for that. In addition to decorating the yard, another custom was the writing on the side of a house so everybody would know in which house a baby was born and whether it was a boy or a girl. Vesna tried to explain to the boys that the yard should be decorated when a mother and her baby were coming back from the hospital, but she quickly gave up and just forbid them to go through with ideas such as burning the tires, writing anything on the house, and similar pranks that used to be a part of the tradition connected with the birth of a child. Perhaps in some parts of Croatia, it was still common to write on the houses, but not on Vesna's house. That was why Viktor's drunken friends came up with a better solution. Nine of them decided to write on their stomachs what they would usually write on the house. They lined up in front of Viktor and took turns turning around so he could witness their masterpiece. When they all turned around, they formed a well-known proverb:

Da je tata imao veći klin, rodio bi se sin.[30]

After a few hours of sleep, Viktor woke up in his old room and quickly got ready to go see his wife and daughter. He went out to the backyard where Vesna and Mate were clearing up the pieces of white cloth and the rest of the evidence of everything that had happened last night.

---

29   One of a family of mandolinlike stringed instruments of southern Slavic regions

30   TN: If the dad had a bigger gun, it would've been a son.

- Sorry about this.

- Go see your child – dad said, motioning toward the door. Viktor smiled, kissed his mother, and headed to the hospital. Along the way, he bought a flower bouquet, peanut puffs, and a yogurt. The visiting hours were actually just one hour long, so he stayed with Nora and Jana the entire time. Jana was sleeping, and her mom and dad did not stop looking at her. How could they not look at something so perfect? Nora told him about how they had brought Jana in, that morning, for Nora to breastfeed her. She described to him how strange it had felt and that nothing worked properly. She somehow managed to come to the conclusion that Jana did not love her because they had not clicked. Viktor had to laugh at that.

- I have a feeling you'll click eventually.

After three days, they were released from the hospital. Viktor brought everything Nora had told him to, although he had been sure he would forget something. They put Jana in a baby nest and, for the first time as a family of three, headed to their apartment. Monika, meanwhile, turned their apartment into a candy factory. She decorated every wall in there, made pink cookies, put out pink balloons and pink signs, and everything else that she could think of. Vesna, Mate, Marija, and Stjepan were also there, eagerly waiting. When Viktor carried Jana into the apartment, all of her grandparents momentarily stopped breathing. He had placed her in the crib, and they watched her without saying a word. They unanimously concluded that they had never seen more beautiful blue eyes, cuter nose, nicer cheeks, sweeter mouth and head in their lives. As small as a pea, she continued to sleep. There is something about children that makes everybody smile. Such a small creature that has nothing but goodness and peace inside has to melt your heart completely, and if that little being is, on top of that, your granddaughter, it is pretty clear that child is the most extraordinary child in the world. Stjepan looked at his own child the same way. He kept going after Nora and hugging her. He was so proud of her, and his heart was bursting with love.

Nora took Jana and went to the bedroom to feed her. Stjepan, Mate, and Viktor went to the balcony, and Vesna and Marija went with Nora.

They helped her change and get comfortable, as well as feed Jana and put her to sleep. It was hard, and it hurt her, but having them there made it a lot easier. Nora thought there was something wrong with her for not being able to breastfeed her own baby, but her mom calmed her down and said it was completely normal.

- It will take time for her to learn how to eat, and you are here to help her with that.

After Jana fell asleep, Nora told them about the childbirth and everything that happened afterward. Everything she was expecting to happen and everything that did happen, but had never before crossed her mind before. Her mom answered all of her questions. After absorbing so much information, she wondered if she had it in her to be a parent. She fell asleep, and Vesna and Marija carefully left the room, letting her rest. They made lunch. In fact, they prepared so much food that Viktor and Nora would not have to cook anything for at least four days. As night fell, it was time to go home. It was hard for Stjepan to leave, and Nora began to cry for her mommy. She knew that was just a hormonal reaction, and that everything was going to be alright, but she wanted her mom to stay, period. It was definitely one of the hardest things Marija ever had to do – leaving her daughter with a little baby, so far away…

- Just call, and mommy will be here in two hours. Night or day – she whispered in her ear and kissed her forehead. Stjepan left an envelope under Jana's pillow and once again kissed the world's most perfect being. He really could not believe that it was possible to feel such love, and all she had to do was look at him with those blue eyes. Every little movement Jana would make seemed more astonishing than the one before.

Mate also left an envelope with money under his little

granddaughter's head. According to tradition, money is placed under a child's head to provide them with a good start in life. And that was it. Viktor, Nora, and Jana were finally alone. They sat next to the crib and just looked at their daughter peacefully sleeping. They could not believe the two of them had created something so perfect. Viktor felt gratitude he had never felt before. He was thankful for Jana, and everything else followed. He felt grateful that he met Nora, that she liked him, that she agreed to be his, and that she wanted him to be hers. He was thankful for the life they had and the people around them. Nora could feel all of it. She could feel how much he cared for her and how much he loved her. She could feel the extent of love he had for their daughter. Their little girl would have everything she needed because there was not anything her dad would not do for her. Viktor lifted Jana out of her crib and walked around their living room. It was the most beautiful sight Nora had ever seen in her life.

They both spent the first night half-awake. They would wake up every two hours so Jana would eat, to change her, or to put her back to sleep. Nora was so tired that she could feel it in every part of her body, but she did not care. She would wake up to every sound coming from the crib, and every time she would go to see if everything was okay. Viktor wanted to help her relax, get some rest, but without much success. Even when he was the one getting up to change Jana, Nora found some excuse – she just had to go to the toilet or drink water. He would laugh every time. She knew what he was trying to do, but she just could not help it. Viktor's coworkers and Nora's college friends visited them daily. Viktor's mom and dad did not want to be in their way, but every day they managed to think of something they had to tell them or bring them. But, none of that bothered Viktor and Nora. They enjoyed witnessing everyone's adoration for Jana. Nora's parents demanded photographs daily, and Nora had a feeling that the whole situation was slowly turning to a live stream from their apartment.

- Do you think it's possible? To set up a camera, just for us to watch Jana – her dad asked her on the phone.

- No, dad — she laughed — You're going to visit us soon, anyway.

The days went by, and Nora and Viktor were slowly learning the ropes. Some days they would think they are killing it as parents, but then Jana would start crying for no reason. In those moments, their minds would go to the other extreme. They were able to come up with a conclusion that their child clearly did not like them, and they were not sure if this would work at all. The good thing was that those mood swings did not happen to them at the same time. Nora got used to breastfeeding, as did Jana, and slowly but surely, they found their rhythm. They somehow managed to get everything done, but the fatigue and exhaustion took their toll. They would not get into huge fights because both of them tried to be understanding, but they were undoubtedly each other's venting outlets. After getting into an argument about some silly thing, with both parties fully aware of how stupid it was, still, it was the hardest thing to calm down.

- Could you please bring me that white gauze?

- Here you go.

- White, Viktor. This is blue.

- Whatever, Nora.

There was that exact tone, as well as the way of pronouncing her name that she could not stand. Especially when Viktor was doing it, and especially when she was not in a good mood. Today was one of those days, and he had just pronounced her name that way.

- Well, it's not whatever — she said, laid Jana down in her crib, and demonstratively took the white gauze herself. Viktor went to the balcony. That was his way to calm himself down before he said something or reacted in a way that would only stir up a fight. He held his hands on his face and breathed in the fresh air. He was tired because they had not slept at all last night, and there was still a lot of work to do. Given that he worked with his dad, he could take some time off to be at home, but he still had to do some of the work. He was barely keeping up with it, but they had all come through for him, so the least he could do was his part. He calmed down, went inside, looked at sleeping Jana, and went to the kitchen, where Nora was washing dishes. He approached her from behind and wrapped his arms around her waist. He kissed her gently on the neck and whispered in her ear.

- I'm sorry. I'm just tired. Go lie down, I'll clean up. I have nothing else to do right now anyway.

Nora turned around and kissed and hugged him. Then, for a few minutes, she just stayed in his arms.

10

The hustle and bustle took over the apartment since the early morning. The guests kept arriving, and Viktor tried to welcome and serve all of them, as Nora prepared Jana and herself for the christening. Although most of the guests announced themselves coming either to the church or the lunch, a few of them who had to travel longer had arrived earlier. Their little apartment was soon crowded, and everyone, of course, wanted to see Jana. Nora retreated to the bedroom to breastfeed and get ready, but someone would keep coming in. Despite all of that, she decided not to stress over anything. Everyone seemed to be having a good time, and that was the most important thing today. Nora's and Viktor's parents were among the first to come so they could help prepare everything. With them, they brought jewelry for their granddaughter so she could have a memory of them and of this day.

Monika was helping, or rather, thought she was helping by welcoming everyone and introducing herself as Monika, Jana's godmother. Besides that, she did not do much.

*

- We met Monika, am I right? – Sofija interjected.

- Oh, that's right. I kind of forgot that you two were there – Nora said, motioning to Veronika and Sofija.

- Well, everything was a little bit hectic. We didn't even have a chance to talk properly. We were late to church, and couldn't really stay long for lunch – Veronika said, stopping herself mid-sentence.

- I remember this nerd researching who Saint Roch was because that was the name of the church. She discovered he was some plague guy.

- Patron saint of plague, Veronika. He was invoked against the plague; you get it?

- Yeah, yeah, that. I found it funny for some reason.

- Oh, my God, I remember that cake. It was some dark chocolate perversion – Sofija recalled and opened her eyes like a little kid who just saw a new toy.

- Now I regret not coming. If you still remember that cake, I can only imagine what it was like.

They all laughed at Ema's comment. She really did feel bad; she remembered that she had had an obligation that could not put off. At that time, they were not keeping up with each other that often, but they always assumed that for such occasions, they would come together.

- We planned that lunch at the last moment, but everything turned out great in the end. The place I wanted was already booked, so Vesna arranged a hotel very close to the church. I even managed to eat, thanks to my dad. Whenever I turned to see where Jana was, he was holding her in his arms or subtly trying to take her from someone else. I don't think I've ever seen him so happy.

*

The christening went great. Although Nora was not as religious as Viktor and his family were, she could see something beautiful in that ceremony. Adopting a child into a community of faith seemed like a pillar of support that her daughter can count on. Jana did not cry, but all the while, she curiously gazed at the priest, following his every movement. Dressed in a small white winter outfit, she resembled an angel. Monika was proud that they had chosen her as Jana's godmother. The feeling of knowing that she would always be this little girl's friend and someone who would always be by her side meant a lot to her. She loved Jana as her own, and it was an exceptional honor to hold her during the christening. There was a connection, which Monika could not describe, but she knew it would last forever. She would always be someone Jana can turn to. That was the promise she made in front of all of these people, and she was planning on keeping it.

Most of the guests left soon after lunch. Nora's parents were among the last ones to leave. Marija found it very hard to say goodbye every time they would have to get going. It was an extraordinary feeling - becoming a grandmother. You love your kids more than anything in the world, but when your baby has a baby, that is exceptional. Even though Marija and Stjepan would feel like they were leaving their own child every single time, Nora never felt like they were really gone. Everyone was giving her advice and ideas about doing something differently or better, but the only opinion that mattered was her mom's. Every time she would have a problem or a question, she would call her mom. And mom always had the answer. Nora hoped that one day she would be able to do the same for her Jana. She was grateful that Viktor's parents lived close by because she knew she could always count on them as well. All in all, she had an excellent team for raising a baby girl.

It has been seven months since Jana was born, and both Viktor and Nora have slowly adapted to the schedule set by Jana. It was tiring to follow her rhythm and lead an "adult" life, but they did not complain. They relished in every moment, mesmerized by Jana every second of the way. Just like parents should be. According to her arm movement and undefined sound emission, they concluded that they are dealing with pure talent, intelligence, and an indisputable genius. After a while, they also learned how to get Jana to not wake up so often, so they had more energy. Viktor returned to his job, so Nora had to get used to being alone with Jana until the afternoon, but soon they found their rhythm.

- Hi, girls.

Viktor returned early from work, with flowers and a lunch he picked up on the way. He still did those little things, which would make Nora feel amazing. He had an incredible ability to make her feel special.

- Hi, lunch boy. We are happy to see you – she laughed and kissed him. She was amazed by how sometimes she would still feel that tingling sensation from head to toe when he kissed her. Isn't it a privilege to find something like that?

- Thank you for the flowers.

- Always. What's up? How is my love? – he picked up Jana from her crib and kissed her gently on the forehead.

- Well, you know, dad, today was a blast. I woke up, ate, then filled up my diaper. And then, a grand finale. I dined again, went to sleep, and made sure my mom got another small gift – Nora was saying in what was supposed to resemble a baby-voice.

- It seems like your mom went absolutely bonkers, don't you think? I'm so sorry you have to deal with her all day long – he turned to Nora, who was sitting at the table and eating lasagna that he had brought straight from the container.

- How was work? Meeting went well?

- Yes, more than well. I got a job offer.

- Really? What?

- Our Dutch partners, who were at the meeting, offered me to come and lead a quality assurance team.

- And what do you think about that? Wait, they offered you this in front of your dad?

- Yeah, he was also taken by surprise a bit. What do we think about it, you ask? Well, Jana just spat on my shoulder, so I think it's pretty clear what she thinks about it.

- What did they offer you? What did you tell them?

- I told them I have to talk to you first. It's an excellent position, and it's well-paid too, but it's a four-year contract. I would come home every six months for a month. I mean, it would be great for my career, but...

- But?

- But I'm not sure if I'm ready to miss four years – he looked at her with Jana in his arms. She knew that look. She knew that his career was important to him and that he loved his work, but she also knew that the two of them were more important to him. Viktor was the type of person who, when he loved something or someone, he loved to the fullest. Likewise, that extreme would also occur if someone was to betray or hurt him. He would not get over those things quickly, and he was ready to give up a lot if he felt hurt or attacked. That trait of his was the biggest mystery to Nora because he was not the person who always had to be right. He was the first to admit he was wrong if that was the case, but he did not forgive easily.

- I am sure.

- Of what?

- That you absolutely don't want to miss four years. The decision will ultimately be yours to make, and whatever you decide, you know everything will be fine.

- I know, yes, thank you. I think I am already a lot more inclined not to go, but I will think about it some more just to make sure I don't regret anything later.

- There, agreed. Anyway, my mom and dad called, they wish to come over for the weekend. You're available?

- I am, yeah, that would be great. Even the weather should be nice, so we can go for a walk somewhere.

Marija and Stjepan arrived on Saturday morning as planned, with breakfast in their hands. Marija once again filled their car with food so that her poor kids would not, by any chance, be hungry. Nora was making coffee while her mom was explaining what she had brought and how to prepare a chicken with all that stuff. Of course, at that point, Stjepan already had Jana in his arms. Marija and Stjepan had a great relationship with Nora, so that was passed to Viktor as well. He loved them visiting because their company was always pleasant and comfortable. He noticed that Nora's dad did not like him at first, so he kept trying to impress him and show him how much he loved his daughter. When one friend told him that a classmate had gotten a son and that he and Jana would probably hang out and go to school together and maybe even get married, he understood Stjepan's feelings about how no one was worthy of his daughter instantly. This time, Stjepan asked him to go look at a car he saw on a classified ads website. Maybe he was starting to like him after all.

- Dad's on the Internet? – Nora asked her mom, surprised that dad was giving in to new technology.

- Oh, my, don't mind him. I've had it up to here with that Internet of his. We could take a walk while they are dealing with that?

- Yes, give a second to dress Jana, and we can go.

- Can her grandma take care of that?

- Well, of course, she can.

There was a small playground near the apartment, which was

always packed as soon as the first rays of sunshine would peek through the clouds. Even though it was March, the temperatures were pleasant, so the children were already out playing or taking a walk with their parents. Swings, merry-go-rounds, slides, and jungle gyms in every color imaginable drew the children in to play. Nora and her mom walked around the playground for a while, then sat on a bench. Jana was happy to be in a stroller; in all the excitement, she fell asleep within three minutes. This was a perfect moment for Nora to spend some quality time with her mom.

- How you've been, my daughter?

- Oh, I'm fine, mom, really. Everything's starting to come together. It's getting easier, I just need to get some sleep, and I will be perfect – she said, laughing.

- And how do you and Viktor get along?

- Great. There is some occasional tension, but the essential parts are amazing.

- That's what's important. You have to work through those small issues right away, and then everything else will be fine. Still, be understanding of my son-in-law. You can be difficult from time to time.

- Great, mom. Thanks – she said sarcastically, raising her head, pretending to be upset.

- You're welcome. Is everything going well with his parents as well?

- Sometimes I'm not really sure how to deal with his mom. I mean, she is accommodating. Whenever I need anything, she is happy to take care of it, whether doing something for me or helping me, but I don't think she is really fond of me. I am trying to be respectful and not talk back to her, but sometimes she goes a bit too far. You know well yourself that I will call regarding every little thing if I need to, but if Viktor and I want to do something a certain way, I don't want her telling me we're doing it wrong. I feel bad about starting an argument with her because I don't want to put Viktor in an awkward situation, but sometimes I really want to answer back to her.

- Look, Nora, opinion about what and how you should be doing something can come from me, or her, or a random person on the street, but that doesn't mean you should or must take that advice and implement it. She is Viktor's mother, and of course, you have to show her respect, but disagreeing does not have to mean disrespecting. The only thing that should matter is the way you communicate. Do you think you would let it slide if Viktor treated your dad or me arrogantly and rudely?

- Well, of course not.

- You see. That's his family. And whatever it's like, now it's yours too. And mine – she told her and hugged her.

It was getting colder, so they headed back to the apartment. There was a store on their way back, so Marija bought everything she needed for the lunch she was planning to cook. She did not really care about Nora's suggestions, she had her own plan. And when she thought about, Nora realized she did not actually mind it either. If mom wants to cook, even better for her. They returned to the apartment before Viktor and Stjepan, who did not arrive until the lunch was already ready. They all had lunch, then spent some more time together, playing with Jana. Nora loved seeing them enjoy themselves with Jana. They acted like little kids. They could not wait for Jana to grow up more so they could bring her to Kutina and show their granddaughter to everyone they knew. They had another coffee together, and just like that, it was already time for Marija and Stjepan to go back to Kutina. Nora hated that part. As much as she was aware they would start annoying each other if they all lived together, every time they would go home, she could not help but feel very sad.

- Come on, love, give me a smile. I'll tell you what your dad and I talked about if that will cheer you up.

- Oh, Viktor, don't be ridiculous. You're going to tell me that anyway – she said and sat down on the couch.

They gave Jana a bath and put her to sleep. The day was exhilarating for her too, so she fell asleep quickly; Viktor and Nora were, surprisingly, in a mood to watch some movie.

- I picked a movie right up your alley – Viktor said, approaching the couch with popcorn and Cedevita[31]. He played the movie, and Nora laughed out loud.

- *The Fault in Our Stars!* Seriously?

- Well, we never finished it.

- True that. Well done, hotshot. You've got the moves.

- Is everything okay? – Viktor asked as Nora kept checking her phone.

- Yeah, yeah.

At that moment, someone rang the doorbell.

- Your folks? – asked Nora.

- I doubt it; it's too late. Maybe a delivery guy can't get in the building or something. Hang on.

Viktor got up and checked the peephole. It was not the intercom; somebody was in front of their door. Nora went to check if Jana was still asleep.

- Good evening. Does Nora Belajec live here?

- Yes, she's here. Just a moment.

- Can we come in?

- Of course, please.

---

31   A brand of Croatian instant vitamin drink, extremely popular in Croatia

Viktor opened the bedroom door.

- Nora, come. The police are here to see you.

She walked toward the hallway that led from the front door to the living room. She could feel her head throbbing as she realized that her peripheral vision was narrowing. She saw two police officers in the hallway. One was middle-aged, tall, and broad-shouldered. He had a brown mustache with a few gray hairs poking out. The other one was much younger. He looked like he was in training, he was shorter and had acne scars on his face.

- What happened? – too aware of her own heartbeat, she could not move.

The officer started out with an apology. Was that an apology for being here this late, or for being here at all because they obviously were not bringing good news? Anyway, he apologized for having to inform them about a car accident on the E70,[32] near the Novska exit. Nora immediately wanted to interrupt him and ask what happened, but she was not able. She did not hear what he was saying from the ringing in her ears, and she could not say anything herself. The officer began to describe the accident, and she felt Viktor slowly taking her hand.

Her parents were driving in the right lane and used a turn signal to overtake a truck in front of them. A truck driver did not notice them and started passing himself. They did not manage to slow down and brake but rammed into the truck. The car behind them crashed into a pile-up and pushed their car under the truck trailer. According to the police officer, the ambulance arrived at the scene of the accident quickly.

- We are sorry. Your parents were killed.

That. That exact moment. That was the combination of words that completely broke Nora down and destroyed her entire world.

---

32   European route E70 (national motorway A3) in Croatia

11

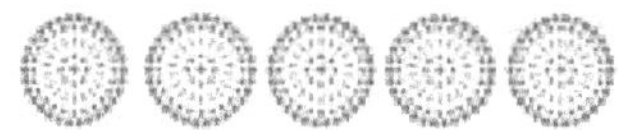

Željko has been a police officer for 27 years, and in his job, he had encountered all sorts of things. There were dangerous, challenging, interesting, fun, and exciting situations; if he had to agree to do any of them, just to avoid these ones, he would do it in a blink of an eye. This girl would forever remember his face and appearance, his tone of voice, and the words he spoke to her. Most people would know exactly what was about to happen when the police would come to their door and start talking to them in the way he just had to, but no one could ever face it. Everyone would always wait for him to say it out loud, and then he was the one responsible for their whole world crumbling.

Nora was sitting on the couch for the last hour, staring blankly ahead. Viktor was right next to her, quiet. Jana woke up, so he went to calm her down. He was not sure if Jana's crying made the situation more difficult for Nora or not, but he did not want to take any chances. He put Jana to sleep again and found Nora still just sitting there. Tears were streaming down her face, but she was not making any sound. Complete silence. In a loss for words, Viktor just hugged her. There were no words that would make sense of anything at that moment. He just held her, letting her cry her heart out. He heard Jana wake up again, and got up to make her a bottle. While he was feeding her, he was trying to think of a way to make all of this easier for Nora, at least a little bit. Nothing occurred to him; probably nothing in this world could lessen the pain she was feeling right now. As he was putting Jana into the crib, he could hear Nora's crying becoming louder. She was lying curled up on the couch. He began to cry with her. It was tearing him apart to see her struggling. If only he could do something, anything. He would give anything right now, just to find a way to ease her pain.

Nora could not get herself together. She expected at least some images playing in her head, but nothing was happening. Only dull pain. Tears were just running down her face out of control, but her head was completely empty. She felt as if she was consciously losing the ability to feel. Maybe that was just her brain, protecting her from outright breakdown. She could feel physical pain all over her body, nausea, and pressure in her chest. At any attempt of calming down, the officer's words would come right back, and the whole process would start again. She wanted to move but did not know where to or how. It was as if all her bodily functions just shut down in one second. She was not aware of where she was or what was happening. She was not aware of Viktor's presence, or his touch. She was not aware of herself.

- Nora, please, just tell me you can hear me. Please, tell me if I can do anything. Please…

She looked at him with the saddest eyes he had ever seen. She heard him.

- Okay, we are not going anywhere – he said, still holding her.

In the morning, Viktor began doing what he could. He informed Monika about what had happened, as well as his parents. He let them know they were going to go to Kutina for a couple of days, wishing to never have to be the bearer of such news ever again. After getting Jana ready and packing up some things they would need for those few days, he found Nora standing in front of the closet, weeping.

- You need help?

- I have nothing black. This must be a mistake, Viktor. It wasn't meant to happen this way, it doesn't make any sense.

- I know, honey.

- Don't you think this was a mistake? Please, let it be a mistake.

Viktor did not say anything. If he had ever wished for something with every fiber of his being, it was for her to be right. There was no strength left in his body to say a single word. She was suffering, falling apart, and what could he do? Nothing. There were no words that could help her, and that was exactly what he had promised her to do. To always look after her and make her feel good. And by every minute that had passed, he kept on breaking that promise.

He laid out dark blue pants and a black T-shirt he had found in the closet for her to put on. Nora sat in the back seat next to Jana and took her hand in hers. The radio automatically started playing as Viktor turned the key, so he quickly turned the volume all the way down. He did not know how to act. He was tiptoeing around her, and that was something he had never had to do before.

- Leave the radio on – she said, clutching at his shoulder.

The trip to Kutina took two and a half hours. Jana slept for the majority of that time; when awake, she looked out the window. This was her first trip to Kutina.

They drove through the plains of Slavonia. Looking at the fields and pastures, it was apparent, even from a plane surface, what a beautiful sight it must be when viewed from up in the air. A breath-taking patchwork of nature. Since coming to Slavonia, Nora was fascinated by all the endless views. This land had some transcendent charm and significance. It was hard to look at all that opulence and not feel gratitude or serenity. As always, they made a stop at Staro Petrovo Selo. Viktor went to the toilet and the store. He asked Nora if she wanted anything, but she just shook her head.

- Nora, you haven't eaten anything. At least drink some water, please. I know you don't care right now, but I can't let you get sick.

- Fine.

- Okay, now that we've got that settled, can I ask you to eat a piece of the sandwich too? – he tried to sound sympathetic but immediately felt foolish. However, Nora did take the sandwich and took two bites.

The change in landscape revealed that they were now in the Moslavina.[33] The road was surrounded by forests and, although they were not yet as green as they were known to be, they were majestic. Marija and Stjepan adored this region. They enjoyed all of its customs, traditions, and nature that, according to their words, offered everything a person would need for happiness in one place. Viktor started thinking about Marija and Stjepan. It was still inconceivable to believe what had happened. He was exposed to news stories about road accidents as everybody else, but he rarely thought about how unexpected that must be for any family who would lose someone like that. You could be sorry, you could sympathize, but you could not understand. It was really absurd how your day could go on as if nothing had happened when you read in the newspaper that someone you did not know was killed in a car accident. It was unbelievable for him to imagine that for someone, today had gone on as if nothing had happened.

The policeman's description of the accident came back to his mind. An unfortunate set of circumstances and a moment of inattention had changed so many lives forever. Then, a thought that made him momentarily panic passed through his mind. In just a few kilometers, they would be driving by the spot of yesterday's accident. How could he be so stupid?!? Why did he not get off the highway? What if the evidence of the crash was still on the road? Nora would not be able to handle that. According to the officer's description, the accident happened near the Novska exit. Perhaps it happened after the exit; he could get off at Novska and avoid the location. The next few minutes, he was driving in a state of sheer panic. He was gripping the steering

---

33   A microregion in Croatia, with Kutina as its main city

wheel, his forehead beaded with sweat. Then he noticed the skid marks on the road, as well as the remainder of shattered glass and headlights. He immediately looked at Nora in the rearview mirror, hoping she did not realize what they had just passed. She did. The expression of pain and anguish on her face was something Viktor was afraid he would never get out of his mind. She squeezed her eyes shut so hard as if she wanted to see the darkest darkness in the world, biting her clenched fist to prevent a scream. Tears streamed down her face, and you could tell she was screaming inside. The pain made Viktor completely break down in a second.

They arrived at Nora's house. Two windows facing the street were surrounded by ivy that Nora's mother would always embellish with flowers in spring. Their home in Kutina was known as the flower house. In front of it, there was a small fountain and an iron fence, while the lower part of the facade had a colored rim about a half a meter high. Every year, Nora and Marija would paint the fountain, fence, and rim in a different color. It was something they enjoyed doing together. This year, everything was blue. To the right of the house was the entrance to the backyard, and the garden followed. They had the walnut, plum, and apple tree planted in their yard. They were maintained and cherished by Stjepan. In the summer, he could sit in the shade of the trees for hours, snoring. Marija took care of the garden. Planting straight rows, plowing, watering, picking, digging, and everything else that would contribute to producing the most delicious produce every single year. Right now, the garden seemed ready for the warmer days in which preparations for Marija's love and care would begin. Nora adored her house and its location. Near the Healthcare Center and the park, it was only ten minutes away by foot to her school, city center, and library.

She found the keys in the same old place. They went in, fed Jana, and put her in a rocking chair. Nora went back to the car to get their things when she encountered her neighbor Branka, an old grandmother she adored. She could make honey or *rakija* from everything and anything she would find in the yard. Of all the flavors she had tasted over the years, Nora's favorites by far were the pine-needle honey and rose honey.

- Nora, baby, is that you?

- Yes, auntie Branka, hi.

Nora just got out of the car, leaving her bag on the side of the road to greet her neighbor.

- Oh, God, don't tell me it was them at Novska – said her neighbor when she realized Nora was wearing black, that her eyes were red from crying, and that this child was battling great grief.

Nora just nodded and burst into tears once again. Auntie Branka hugged her as tight as she could, weeping together with her.

*

- Terrible. I got chills – Dajana said.

- I'm so sorry you had to go through all of that. It was only later that I found out what had happened – Veronika also interjected.

- Well, you couldn't have known. Seriously. I know, it's surprising for Kutina, but that is why I wanted to deal with everything in one day. So I wouldn't have to let everyone know. I knew that was my mom and dad's wish. That is, I was familiar with their feelings about funerals. Also, if I had decided to contact one person, I would have to reach everyone too.

- I know, but anyway. I'm sorry we weren't there for you.

- Don't get me wrong, but I wasn't even aware of it then. Viktor and Jana were there with me, and Monika came to help with the organization. I only contacted my mom's and dad's brothers. It really was only immediate family, along with a couple of friends they used to see every day. My parents found funerals to be a real pain in the ass. They saw them as too much money spent on candles and flowers that nobody has any use of.

*

Despite not knowing his way around Kutina, Viktor set out on a search to find a grocery store so he could buy food and drinks for a small wake they were organizing. Monika looked after Jana and prepared everything in the house, while Nora and Viktor went to arrange a funeral. They arranged everything for the day after tomorrow.

During the wake, Nora sat in an armchair and stared at the piano in the living room. Here in the house, she could not get memories of mom and dad out of her head. She pictured mom sitting at the piano, remembering how dad enjoyed listening to her playing. They both adored music, and Nora was sure the music was what brought them together. Their dancing was not perfect, but when they danced together, they looked beautiful. Nora reminisced on their family's movie nights as well. Her parents were just not good at it at all. They would talk so much during a movie that everything was just pointless. You could not even ask them about the plot, because their versions of what was happening or about to happen never matched the actual movie version. They both had their own quirks, but they learned how to deal with each other. At the end of the day, it all came down to the fact that they really truly and unconditionally loved each other.

Not a lot of people gathered in the house on Sunday night. But Nora's heart was full because of all the genuine embraces. Now, she was listening to stories about her parents in the past tense, and every now and then, her eyes would tear up. Her emotions were all over the place. Regardless of feeling numb and empty, she took joy in listening to all those stories. Experiencing her parents through other people's eyes, she felt proud to be their child.

The funeral was arranged for Tuesday. Viktor made sure everything was exactly as she said it should be. He invited people she wanted there and did not post any obituaries. A small group of people gathered at the cemetery as the ceremony was about to be conducted by a priest who was a family friend. According to tradition, Nora, Viktor, her mother's brother, and all of her father's brothers were standing in the morgue with the bodies, while other guests would come in to express their condolences. Viktor decided to keep the coffins closed. He did not want that to be the way Nora would remember her parents forever. The priest arrived, and everything was ready for the coffins to be taken out. They were placed side by side. Together.

Behind the coffins stood Nora with Viktor, and behind them were her parents' brothers with their families. The priest began the prayer. He talked about the way the Church interpreted death, but Nora did not hear any of it. She repeated prayers along with the others, but in fact, she just stared at the coffins in front of her. She could not believe that she was saying goodbye to her mom and dad. How would she ever find solace?

At one point, the priest began to talk about Marija and Stjepan. How he loved their company, and about the positive energy they both radiated and that was utterly infectious. He expressed how honored he was to know them. The procession began its way to the gravesite, preceded by the priest, followed by the coffins, family, men, then women. Viktor held Nora the entire time, afraid she might completely fall apart if he let her go, even for just a moment. Everyone was explicitly asked not to bring any flowers; Viktor made sure to have one red rose ready for everyone. It was her mom's favorite flowers. That was his way to respectfully say goodbye to them. He promised Nora that after the funeral, he would let the others know what had happened. Many of them were angry that they did not have the opportunity to say goodbye, and he could understand that. On the other hand, he tried to explain to them that Nora had organized the funeral the way Marija and Stjepan would have wanted.

When they reached the gravesite, the priest began another prayer. Nora shut herself off again. She imagined her mom cooking lunch and her dad playing with Jana, wishing they were here now. It was too difficult to say goodbye. She just could not imagine life without them. She could not conceive them missing every significant moment in her life, or Jana not remembering them. Her not being able to call mom whenever she needed her advice, or her daddy not being there, protecting her from everyone. It was just unthinkable to imagine she would never see them again.

She was thinking about the accident. About that damn second that led to her standing by her parents' grave, throwing a pile of earth at their coffins. She thought about their last moments. Were they able to find peace in being together?

She also thought about her mom's last birthday. Dad must have gotten her a red rose; the same one people are now throwing in their grave. Nora was on the verge of breaking down. She needed to scream, do something, anything. Being alone and quiet with her thoughts was going to make her mad. The invisible thread holding her together would surely break.

It did break. Nora's painful shriek made everyone around her weep. All her pain, all the sadness, and suffering she let out with that scream echoed beyond the edge of the sky. She broke down as they were lowering her mom, the strongest woman she knew, and her dad, a person with the biggest heart on the planet, down into the ground. The loudest silence floated through the air, blended with Nora's deafening sobs muffled by Viktor's embrace, and the melody coming from a single guitar. Some boy was playing a song Marija and Stjepan danced to at their wedding, 27 years ago.

Zakuni se, ljubavi, na ramenu mom,

zakuni se, ljubavi, u trenutku tom.

Zakuni se, ljubavi, da moja si sva,

da sanjaš, ljubavi, sve što sanjam ja...[34]

---

34   Translator's note: *Swear to me, my love, here on my shoulder, swear to me, my love, in this moment. Swear to me, my love, to be all mine, to have dreams, my love, the same dreams as I.* (Song by Srebrna Krila – Zakuni se ljubavi)

12

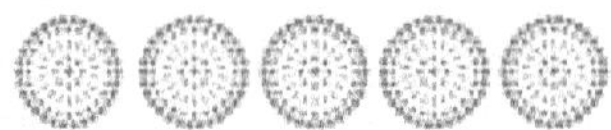

Nora spent another afternoon locked in the bedroom, which was now devoid of any light, even daylight. Darkness suited her. It was the only way for everyone to leave her alone, including her own mind. She dreamed every night. She also dreamed every afternoon while taking a nap. She would dream of disgusting things. Something completely abstract, but it would take all of her energy. She would also dream of either the police officer's voice, the funeral, or the accident, which she had not witnessed, but her damn head kept imagining it. In that dream, she would always see mom and dad sharing a look right before the crash. She was in a vicious cycle in which she had to sleep because she did not have any strength to live, but her dreams exhausted her even more.

It was physically demanding for her to take a step or eat or talk, walk, think. Any action, even the smallest one, made her so tired she could barely keep her eyes open. She was terrified to think, to sleep, terrified of herself. Everything she did, she was doing mechanically. She fed Jana mechanically, she ate and showered mechanically. The feeling of emptiness inside took over her physical body. Sometimes, a slight emotion would come through, her body's desire to shake off the darkness overwhelming her. But nothing would ever change.

She was falling apart in front of Viktor's eyes. Two weeks had passed since the funeral, and Nora barely spoke ten sentences. She was sleeping the entire time, did not eat or speak. Viktor tried everything, but nothing worked. He had never been surrounded by such sadness before, and he did not know how to handle it. He did not know how to help her get out of it.

He stayed home to take care of Nora and Jana, feeling miserable that there was nothing he could do but to leave her alone. Every night when he would lie beside her, he could feel her pain. He would hug her, but with every touch, she would start to cry more. Her tears ached. Her pain and immense sadness hurt.

Between taking care of Jana, letting Nora sleep as much as she wanted, and trying to get her to eat at least something, Viktor also worked from home so he would not have problems at work. His mom told him that the situation was going too far, but he assured her that Nora just needed time to pull herself together. And no matter how long it was going to take, he would be patient. It was up to him to make sure everything else is under control so she could recover. The reason he knew everything was going to be okay was Jana. As hard as it was for Nora to go through this, and for him to look at her like this, he could see the comfort Jana brought to Nora at this challenging time.

*

Vesna frequently came by to help him, and on several occasions, she even tried to talk to Nora, but Nora was asleep every time. Or was she pretending to be asleep, just so she did not have to see anyone? Vesna could hear her crying in the bedroom and wished she could help her somehow. Monika often stopped by, too. Her best friend was going through the most difficult time of her life, and she could not do anything to help. She could just imagine how Viktor must have been feeling. Were they selfish for not wanting to watch her suffer? For thinking how hard it was on them too? Monika would often take Jana for a walk so Viktor could work in peace. He was thankful, but she wished she could do more.

- How is she today? – she asked, getting Jana ready for another walk.

- The same. She's asleep – Viktor answered, shaking his head.

- I don't know what to do, Monika. I'm scared she'll get sick. We struggle every day to get her to eat something, anything. I think she only eats because she's breastfeeding Jana.

- Maybe she should go talk to someone?

- I thought of that, too. I asked her if she thinks talking to a psychiatrist would help. She doesn't want to go. Or anything. She doesn't have to talk to me about it if she doesn't want to, but she has to speak to someone. My mom even suggested a priest.

- Honestly, I wouldn't really say that's the best option when it comes to Nora.

- Yeah, that's what I said, but at this point, I'm open to any ideas.

- I understand that. I'll go ask her again if she wants to take a walk with us. I have nothing to lose.

Monika tiptoed into the bedroom, but then midway changed her mind about being quiet. Even if Nora was asleep, it was time for her to wake up; if she was pretending, sneaking in did not make any sense, anyway. Monika left the room two minutes later.

- Okay, she doesn't want to – she said sadly.

Monika walked around with Jana for about an hour before returning to the apartment. She told Viktor that it was high time to kick some sense into Nora and get her back to normal. At least more normal than her current state. Monika suggested him to stop working from home and go back to his regular routine because that would make Nora slowly return to some of her daily responsibilities as well.

- It's great that you take care of everything, but I'm not sure it helps her case – she told Viktor kindly, assuming he was sick of constantly getting unsolicited advice from everybody.

He thought about it while bathing Jana and putting her to sleep. Nora fed her, kissed her, and went back to bed without saying a word to Viktor. He decided to listen to Monika's advice because he realized that the situation was getting worse day by day. But he was still concerned, so his mom agreed on checking on Nora while he was at work.

Determined to find a way to help her, Viktor sat down and turned on his laptop. For nearly three hours, he was reading about recognizing symptoms of depression. Nora did have most of the symptoms he came upon, which made him hopeful that the tips from that article could help. According to a psychologist who went through depression herself, Deborah Serani, there were several ways for Viktor to contribute to Nora's recovery. He decided to follow all of them: being there for Nora, using small gestures to show his love and support, not criticizing or being harsh, not diminishing her pain or offering advice, not comparing her circumstances with someone else's, learning about depression, and having a lot of patience.

His first day back, Viktor was completely unproductive. His mind was with Jana and Nora. Maybe he should have taken Jana to his mother. But then Nora would have spent all day in bed again. This way, she would at least have to take care of Jana. At least she would get up. He left work early and found his mom in their apartment.

- I've only been here for two hours. I just finished cooking lunch.

- Thanks, mom. How is she?

- I don't know. We didn't speak much. I'm leaving, honey. If you need anything, call me.

- I will.

He kissed his mother and went to check on Jana. She was sleeping in her crib. Nora came out of the bedroom and went to the bathroom.

- Hey, love.

- Hey.

- Something smells good in the kitchen. You want to eat?

Nothing. End of conversation. He could only hear the bathroom door closing and the sound of water running. He went to eat something, preparing himself for persuading her to eat something, as well.

*

It has been a month since he returned to work, and every day when he would return home, he hoped Nora would at least smile at him. Look at him, kiss him, talk to him. He missed his wife. But things seemed to be improving. Nora slept less because Vesna was no longer checking in every day. She would take care of Jana, and that was pretty much it. She would spend the rest of the day in the bedroom or in front of the TV, staring more into space than at the screen. Monika kept visiting, but nobody has had a conversation with Nora for longer than five minutes. It was hard for everyone, but they were still understanding.

Viktor could feel that the stress from home was affecting his work. He had a hard time getting the job done, and that was making him angry. He loved his job and had a clear vision of what he wanted to accomplish for as long as he could remember. His work has always been at the highest level, so nobody could ever relate his success with the fact that his dad owned the company. He headed home with high hopes that today was going to be a good day. He took a deep breath, calmed down, and walked through the door.

The apartment was a mess, the dishes were dirty, and there were still clothes in the washing machine that he had washed last night. Jana just woke up and needed to be changed. When she started crying, Nora walked out of the bedroom, but then she saw Viktor and went back to bed. He lost it. He changed Jana and put her into a little swing.

- Nora? — Viktor walked into the room and opened the window. Fresh air and daylight immediately filled the room, which also needed to be cleaned thoroughly. He sat next to her and lifted her in a sitting position.

- Please, talk to me. If not me, we'll find somebody else, but you have to talk to someone. This has gone too far — he said nicely. He felt terribly guilty about starting to resent her. He did not want to admit it, but all of this was affecting his patience. Of course, that was a wrong attitude to have, but he could not help it. Fatigue and stress had done their part.

Nora was not only sad, but she had also lost herself completely. Her behavior has changed; she did not respond to anything happening around her, and it seemed like she could not keep up with the simplest of conversations. Leaving the bedroom and eating were improvements, but that was some different Nora. She still did not eat enough, she did not speak. She would just answer their questions. She was a definition of a person whose spirit had been entirely broken.

- Nora?

- What do you want?

- Seriously? Can you at least make an effort to speak nicely?

- Viktor, do you need something or…?

- I need you to talk to me normally.

- I am talking normally. Don't act like a brat. If you need something, say it, if you don't, don't be annoying. I don't feel like talking. I am barely holding back from saying all I want to as it is.

- Oh, please, Nora, don't you refrain yourself. I would like to hear it — Viktor said sarcastically. That was a moment when he realized a fight was about to happen, but he could not stop himself. Perhaps he could, but he did not want to.

- Come on, I'm really curious. What are you holding back?

- I should've listened to daddy! I shouldn't have married you. And he told me so. None of this would have happened had we not been married. I wouldn't have stayed in Osijek, they wouldn't have had to come to visit me, and none of this would have happened.

- You gotta be kidding me?!? Nobody forced you to marry me, nobody forced you to stay in Osijek. We decided that together. Actually, why am I even justifying myself, this is ridiculous – Viktor said, and ran out of the apartment.

He was out of energy. Somewhere deep down, he knew that Nora had not meant any of that. She just had to put the blame on someone, but right now, he did not have the strength, wish, or willpower to look for justifications for her behavior.

Nora felt terrible. The new kind of terrible. She meant none of what she had just said. It was her fault. She kept calling her mom, acting like a clueless little kid. She was doing that, knowing exactly that her mom and dad would immediately get in the car and come to her. She was taking advantage of that. If she had not been so spoiled, they would have been alive now. Why was she not the one to get in the car with Viktor and Jana, and visit them, instead of them visiting her all the time?

She did not feel like doing anything, all she felt was being annoyed. Annoyed at Viktor for continually fussing over her, annoyed that he was sending Vesna to check up on her, even annoyed at Monika for acting all cautious around her as if she was mentally ill. Everything was getting on her nerves. She had never felt so tired and never for so long. She would wake up every night and walk around the apartment like a ghost, making her well acquainted with every corner of that apartment. There would be times when she would sit in the bathroom in the middle of the night with sleeping pills in her hands. Those pills were another one of Viktor's attempts to help her. She would look at the dozen pills in her hand, thinking that might be the easy way out. Nobody was better off with this version of Nora, anyway. She was only making Viktor's life more difficult. If she did not snap out of it soon, Jana would suffer too. Nora looked at her daughter, who was peacefully sleeping. That baby was the only thing keeping her alive. She had to come to herself, she had to snap out of it. But in a split of a second, the darkness would overcome her again – the feelings of guilt, anger, sadness. All past moments, which she could now only regret. It was hard not to think about her mom and dad. If she was not thinking about everything they went through together, she was thinking about all the situations that would happen without them being there. All of them seemed grim and dark. She felt the need to explain that pain and darkness to Viktor. If he understood how much it hurt, he surely would not expect her to eat or talk or be in a good mood. But how do you explain something like that?

She was still lying in the room when Viktor returned. A sudden feeling of relief overwhelmed her as soon as she heard him coming in. But that sense of comfort and security would vanish as fast as it appeared; she would give anything if she could only hold on to that feeling for a few minutes longer. Just to try to repair a relationship she had been consciously and intentionally destroying. She cried herself to sleep. Viktor slept on the couch. He lay down two hours after she did; after he had cleaned up the apartment, eaten, put Jana to sleep, and finished preparing for tomorrow's meeting. He was utterly exhausted, both physically and mentally.

The meeting Viktor had been preparing for weeks was running long. It was the last thing he needed; he had already been high-strung all day. He would leave early almost every day to go home, not even able to remember when was the last time he went out for drinks with guys. He turned them down again today. As soon as this meeting was done, he would go home. Sitting on pins and needles, he kept glancing at his watch, trying to speed things up. He did not think that was very obvious until his father apologized to everyone and sent him home. Like he was a child. He was furious. He took his things and left.

*

What awaited him at home, further raised a degree of Viktor's hopelessness. Instead of his family being his safe place and comfort after a hard day at work, he would dread going back home every day. That was the hardest part of his day. Viktor did not want to deal with that atmosphere, did not want to argue, to be ignored. His resentment towards Nora was growing, and he hated it. It made him not wanting to go home at all. A normal person should not feel that way. Well, maybe he was no longer a normal person. He sat in his car for a while. It is hard when you have to take the time out of your day to brace yourself for going to your own apartment and being with your own family. And it is even harder admitting that to yourself.

He could hear Jana crying from the hallway. She had been restless for the last few days, and they could hardly calm her down. Her waking up multiple times a night had done wonders for her already well-disposed and not-at-all sleep-deprived parents.

- Where the hell have you been until now? – Nora asked instead of greeting him as soon as Viktor walked in. He rolled his eyes as he was closing the door behind him.

- My meeting went long – he said with a monotonous voice. After all the countless fights, the lack of reaction to Nora's remarks proved as the best tactic.

- There is always something with you. She's been crying for two hours. Perhaps I would like to have time to do something, too.

- Here you go, Nora, I'll take her, and you go and do something! Do something that doesn't involve lying in a fucking room!

And that was it. The uproar and the confrontation commenced, and the insults were being thrown left and right. It seemed as if the only purpose of it was to lash out at each other and to engage in the competition of who can scream the loudest. Even their quarrels were not making any sense anymore. They were both simultaneously yelling incoherent ramblings at each other. Like two lunatics talking to themselves, but in the same room and facing each other.

- Enough! I heard you shouting from the street. Are you two aware of the fact that your baby is right here and crying?!? – Monika rushed into the apartment after hearing them fight. Many would have stayed in the building corridor to avoid an awkward situation, but Monika was not one of those people. She stared at them in an attempt to embarrass and calm them down. Nora grabbed her sweatshirt from the table and ran out of the apartment, demonstratively slamming the door behind her.

- I see you've started communicating again? – Monika said in a poor attempt to lighten up the mood. But she could not. She should have assumed that, as soon as she heard the words that they had yelled to each other. Such words, coming from a person you love, are sure to cause pain, even kill. Viktor took Jana out of the swing and tried to calm her down.

- Yeah, we're doing great – he said with such sadness in his voice that it almost made Monika cry. She watched him with Jana; she looked so tiny in his arms.

- I'm going after her – Monika said quietly and left the apartment. As she was walking toward the park, she realized how angry she was at Nora. Everyone around her was trying to reach out to her, help her, everyone was there for her, but Nora did not seem to see that. Nora was sitting on a bench with arms around her knees. She was all curled up in a sweatshirt that seemed two sizes too big. In fact, everything on her seemed like it. Monika sat down next to her and just stayed silent for a while. There was so much she wanted to tell her; she was worried, sad, angry, and a hundred other things she could not even define.

- Nora, you've got to pull yourself together.

- Leave me alone, Monika, please – Nora said softly. Tears were streaming down her face, but she was trying to hide it from Monika. Nora did not want her to see them. All she really wanted was for everyone to leave her alone. How to explain to them that she was fully aware of what she was doing, that she saw what she was making them go through, but that she just could not help herself? How to explain that she did not know how was it possible to still have any tears left? Nora could not explain it, so it was better for everyone to just stay away.

- I can't leave you alone. You have to find a way to get better. And if you can't, you have to let us help you.

- You have to start worrying more about your life and leave me alone.

- Don't be rude.

- I'm not any ruder than you who don't seem to understand anything. I don't feel like talking, why do you keep pushing?

- Yeah, I caught on to that, but you'll have to start talking at some point. You are going to ruin all the relationships in your life. Is that what you want? To end up completely alone so you can cry over your fate unbothered? I get it, it's hard. I can't even imagine what you're going through, and I hope I won't ever have to know myself, but your life can't just stop. You can't just switch off. What exactly are you waiting for to happen in that damn room?

- Won't you leave me alone already? I came here so I didn't have to listen to your smart tips on how to forget my mom and dad were dead – she started to raise her voice as if that would scare Monika away.

- Who told you that you should forget that?!? But you also shouldn't forget that you have a baby that needs you to take care of her. And that you have a husband who loves you, but who can't take this anymore.

- Please, keep on explaining these things to me. Because you have both a husband and a child, so you must know everything, right?

- Screw you, Nora. Go on like this, and soon you won't have any of that either.

13

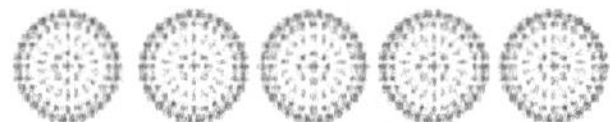

They were sitting at the kitchen counter. Silent. Nora was eating, while Viktor was reading the news on his phone and drinking coffee. Silence became an everyday occurrence in their household. Their life together started to resemble the most mundane movie ever, just sharing a living space and taking care of Jana. Nora's phone began vibrating in the middle of a large wooden counter; her ringtone had been turned off a long time ago. She ignored it.

- You're not going to answer? – Viktor asked with a combination of sarcasm and frustration in his voice.

- If it's important, they'll call again – Nora replied indifferently.

- Unbelievable – Viktor sighed and picked up the phone.

- Hello, Viktor Belajec speaking.

After a few moments of him just listening to the person on the other end of the line, Viktor handed the phone to Nora. She was still taken aback by him even picking up her phone, but like most of her reactions lately, he ignored that one too.

- The lawyer needs you, something to do with the house. Answer and don't act like a big baby.

Nora just took the phone from his hand and went to the bedroom. For twenty minutes, she listened to her lawyer explaining the things her mom and dad had never wanted to bother her with. She was never involved in family finances more than her parents would allow. She was brought up to understand the value of money and to know that she had to earn it through hard work. They were not a wealthy family, but she always had whatever she wanted, as long it was within reason. What she did not know was that the money for her studies, for example, had been obtained from a loan. She also did not know that the student loan was not her parents' only loan, and she felt ashamed that she had never thought about where the money for all her needs came from. The lawyer now explained how her mom and dad had taken out a new loan to refinance all the old ones, but that no payments had been made for a while now. Since they did not leave a will, and Nora was their only child, she was also the sole legal inheritor of everything they had. Their house was put up as collateral, and if Nora could not pay off their debt, it would be put up for public auction so that the loan could be closed and the debt settled.

- Is there any other way to save the house if I can't repay those debts right now? – Nora asked after the lawyer had finished explaining, in the hope she would be able to keep the only physical connection to her parents she had left.

- Unfortunately, no – said the lawyer with a reassuring voice even though he was giving out bad news. – But you can visit the house and pick up some keepsakes. I heard what happened, and I'm truly sorry I can't do more.

- Thank you. And I will definitely go over there this weekend, you can sell the house after that.

Nora hung up and lay on the bed for a few moments. She thought about the house she grew up in, surprised that the news did not affect her as much as she would expect them to. Now that mom and dad were not there anymore, maybe she stopped considering that house to be her home.

She briefly told Viktor that they would put up the house for auction to cover her parents' debts and that she would go to Kutina for the weekend to pick up some things. She did not explain much, and what was worse, he did not really care.

Nora's plan was to go there for two days and take Jana with her, but Viktor was home on the weekends anyway, and he argued she would be done faster without Jana there. Nora got up early on Saturday, got ready, and left the apartment without saying goodbye. Viktor was awake and aware of all of it, but like usual, did not react. He remembered that on one occasion, while they were still just dating, she had told him that saying goodbye was one of the most important things she wanted them to adhere to in their relationship. They agreed that they would never leave each other without a kiss goodbye. Whatever happened, whether they were in a hurry or had a fight one minute earlier. To her, it was a symbol of love and respect. A sign that they were both sure that whatever was going on, nothing can jeopardize what they had. Now, that seemed like some different Nora, because Viktor could not remember the last time they had kissed or been affectionate in any way.

It took Nora two and a half hours to reach Kutina, and she was listening to the radio that entire time. She forgot how much she loved that, and now, as she was getting closer to her old home, she did start to feel a little bit different. She parked in her old yard. It was June, and it was getting warmer outside, so she felt comfortable in a plain light oversized T-shirt and sweatpants. The feeling reminded her of coming home from school and changing into the most comfortable combinations, those you wear "around the house."

Nora made herself some coffee and sat under the walnut tree, so she could enjoy this moment of peace. She looked at her house, where she had spent so many years. All the firsts in her life happened in that house. Birthdays, playtimes, summer and winter holidays, every Christmas, first heartbreak, first permission to go out, first hangover, first arguments; all that happened in that little flower house. The fact that she was losing it did not feel real, but that was exactly what was happening. That house was her mom and dad. They adored it, and Nora loved the way they had made it into a home.

She decided to go through the entire house and take only the things that meant the most to her. Her main and only rule was not to go over the top with the amount of stuff. This was important because Nora had a habit of keeping useless junk just because of some special memory attached to it.

The living room was the same for as long as she could remember. Marija furnished it to her liking and did not allow anyone to change it a lot. Good thing she lived with two people who were not interested in decorating at all. There was a large clock on the wall that Marija adored. It was very detailed and eye-catching, and according to Marija, it matched the chair in the middle of the room. Beneath the clock stood a piano. Marija was always saddened by the fact that Nora was not interested in playing it as much as she was. The same as the needlepoint, which Marija loved to do, while Nora gave up that hobby after about an hour. The two that were hanging on the wall were "A woman reading" and "A boy with a guitar." Two patterns that all mom's friends and relatives had as well. Those two were a must-have if you were serious about your needlepoint. In the corner of the room stood a wood stove that Stjepan cherished. As soon as it would get a little colder, as soon as the first wind would blow or the first rain, which could no longer be called summer rain, would fall, Stjepan would stack the wood and start the fire. Any fruit they had in the house would end up on the top of that stove, so the whole house would smell delicious; apples were his favorite. Nora remembered him sitting with one half of a baked apple and watching some Croatian TV show, eating the middle of it with a little spoon. From a young age, she would love to stand in front of that stove, facing her back to it, and then, when she could no longer withstand the temperature, she would quickly hop on the couch and enjoy the feel of the heat going from her feet to her upper back. Dad taught her that when Nora was little, and they would often goof around like that. The thing she chose to take from the living room was a book that dad gave her mom for one of her birthdays. It was a collection of poems by Sergei Yesenin, who Marija loved, and in it was written a verse: *For you, I choose the sweetest words.*

Their dining table stood between the kitchen and the living room, and on the wall behind it, Stjepan hung photographs of some of the most important events in their lives. On one side, there were photos from mom and dad's and Nora and Viktor's weddings, pictures from Nora's first and last day of elementary school, then the first and last day of high school, the photos of Nora leaving for Osijek, and Nora on her graduation day. Their entire life was on that one side of the wall, while the other side was reserved entirely for photos of Jana. One photo from when she was leaving the hospital, one from the christening, one where she just posed adorably, one only with her grandma, one only with her grandad, one with Nora holding Jana, and one with Marija, Stjepan, and Jana. Nora took down the last one and saw they had written *Our angel's angel* on the back of it. She was sure that it was her dad's choice of words.

The next room was the kitchen, a place where Nora and her mom would often spend time together and talk. Several times they had tried to cook or clean together, but after just a few minutes, they would conclude it would be better if only one of them did it all, and that one should be the mom. Nora would never object. That kitchen was always ready for cooking. Even if a stranger walked in there, they would quickly find everything they needed. The spot Nora particularly loved was the shelf on the window where her mom was keeping all of her spices. Marija believed them to be the secret of good cooking. The thing Nora took from there was her mom's recipe notebook. She had never made a cake from scratch or had a desire to do so, but she adored that notebook. It was full of recipes and full of papers that her mom used to write down recipes on the go. Nora loved the expression on her mom's face before she would choose which cake to bake. She would sit down at the table and go through her notebook as if there were some hidden treasure inside of it. She flipped through that stack of papers from the beginning to the end a thousand times, and every time she would enjoy it like she was a little kid.

Nora left everything she had picked by now on the living room table and went to mom and dad's bedroom. That room was full of light, and there was, of course, a huge double bed. Their wardrobe smelled like them. Nora ran her hand over the clothes hanging on the hangers, and images of her mom and dad popped up in her mind. Everything seemed so unreal. For a moment, she would completely forget why she was in that house right now, what she was doing, and why she was doing it. The house was not giving away the tragedy that had happened to Nora's family, and despite that being their home, Nora did not feel the stifling feeling of depression there. Everything she saw just awakened fond memories of them. It was painful to think that from now on, there would be nothing but those memories, but Nora tried to focus on the fact that she had witnessed the beautiful life Marija and Stjepan had built. She found a photo album, mom's perfume, jewelry, and dad's favorite T-shirt. Those were the things she could not leave without.

There was only her room left. Nora left it for last because she knew what was waiting for her there. Those four walls embodied her entire childhood. She knew every corner and every line of that room. This was where she hid all of her notes and letters from school, where she tried her first cigarette just to see what it was like, put up posters and photographs and wrote down quotes, which were the proof somebody understood what she was going through. Those were the days of adolescent storm and stress, heartbreak, seeking comfort, and seeking motivation. Nora did not know what to take from her room, and that was precisely what she had known would happen. She sat on the floor to look through all the books she had collected over the years when she found a box with a bunch of high school keepsakes.

It took her a second to figure out what that was when she started going through all the notes in the box. These were the notes on which you would write your biggest secret or some gossip during class, then pass it to your friend at the other end of the row. You would fold the paper, pass it on, and then attentively follow its path so it would not end up in the wrong hands or read by the wrong person, for example, a teacher. Aloud. In front of the whole class. Nora remembered one teacher who had particularly enjoyed doing just that. Every time she would see a note, she would pompously ask: *„Couldn't this have waited until the recess?"* Well, it could not. If it could have waited until the recess, then they would have waited until the recess.

Nora was now going through the box full of those kinds of notes. Oh, the disastrous problems they were facing! The entire class would make talk about skipping school on some of those notes, and everyone would write down – *if everyone goes, I go.* And there would always be this one kid who did not want to go. Nora was never that kid. She was looking through those notes and completely lost track of time. They all thought their problems were the worst in the world then. Nora thought about how she would give anything to have those kinds of problems right now, and because of that thought, she immediately felt thirty years older than she really was. There were four notebooks at the bottom of the box, and Nora laughed out loud when she realized what they were.

They were the collections of four years' worth of their high school bloopers and shenanigans.

As soon as she started reading them, she began to remember all those silly situations and statements. She has not laughed that hard for a long time.

*

- Yeah, I remember. You called me that evening – Veronika interjected and turned around to face the rest of the girls – That's when I told you about her parents.

- I felt awful. My parents mentioned something about that accident, but somehow I thought I would have already found out if that were your parents.

- I know that we were sure it could never happen to us, to lose contact as we have, but we really did go our separate ways. When I found those notebooks, I could not remember when was the last time I heard from or saw any of you. That's why I called you – Nora explained.

- In those notebooks, was there anything about that time when Filip during the third period realized that he'd forgotten his bag? Like, he didn't even need it until the third period – Ema remembered, and girls started laughing out loud. Sofija had just taken a sip of beer, and it almost flew out of her mouth, so the laughing continued.

- There were a lot of situations that I completely forgot about, but some of them made me laugh so hard I cried. Do you remember that physics professor, the one that always had that creepy smile? One time he talked about how only the speed of thought was faster than the speed of light, and then Luka wisely concluded that was really true because first, you had to think about turning the lights on, and only then you can turn it on.

- I remember when Ema got unexcused absence.

- Oh my God, yes, and it wasn't my fault at all. We were supposed to have a free period after the lunch break, but then someone informed us that the class was happening after all. But we wisely concluded it could've very easily happened that we just didn't get the message.

- Yeah, and then our homeroom professor asked you where you were, and you fool said you overslept. The fourth period! Like, you were there for the first three periods, but then you miraculously overslept the fourth one.

- Well, I panicked and didn't know what to say – they all started laughing so much that even the waiter smiled, watching them genuinely having fun. He sent them another round on the house.

- That evening when we spoke on the phone and talked about these gags, that was the first time since the funeral that I felt any peace. I decided to take a walk around the town and go to the mom and dad's grave for the first time. I went up Church Street and realized how physically exhausted I was from all the sadness that had haunted me since their deaths. I remember I shivered when I saw their names on the crosses, but somehow I calmed myself down, greeted them, sat by the edge of the grave, and started talking. It may sound a bit disturbing, but it was really nice. I could visualize their faces and imagine everything they would say in response, so that relaxed me. Or *they* did, I'm not sure.

*

It was already dark outside, and the cemetery was illuminated by a thousand lanterns and candles. Nora spent a few moments just watching the lights before she headed home. She walked around the city she grew up in, and the longer she was away, the more she started to miss it. Every corner of Kutina reminded her of something.

Her favorite part of the city was the *porches*[35] on Church Street. Every day while passing there on her way to the elementary school, she would be in awe of them. That was an ensemble of five houses built of oak beams and planks in the traditional architectural style at the turn of the 20th century. In her mind, she had one family housed in each of those houses, and that had become her daily pastime. She would imagine what their lives looked like and how they spent their days.

---

35   Also called *Trijem* (eng. Porch)

Tena Grgić – The Porches of Moslavina

Nora spent countless hours in the city library, digging through the shelves, thinking to herself that she must be crazy for spending her time there rather than going shopping with the girls. She shared her first ice cream with a boy in the ice cream shop nearby. And because he paid 3 kuna[36] for her scoop, Nora and her group of friends automatically considered him the real man, unlike the other immature boys. He was nine. Nora walked past the court and recalled a bistro where they used to eat *lepinjas*[37]. They would not order ćevapi[38] like normal people, but just *lepinjas*. After she walked around for a bit, Nora decided to sit in front of her high school. There was no one there, so she lay down on the bench and looked at the stars. She tried not to think about anything. Her mind was completely empty, and she had never been happier about it.

The thought of her daughter crossed her mind; she missed Jana. Nora wondered if she would be able to give Jana the childhood that her mom and dad had given her. But she realized there was nothing in this world that would stop her from providing that child with everything she deserved. The thought of losing this house still saddened her, especially because she would never be able to show Jana her grandparent's home. But Nora promised to herself that Jana would meet them through her eyes and her stories. Nora thought about Viktor, too. She was aware that she was making his life difficult, but she did not feel guilty. Maybe because she knew that everything has to pass at some point or another.

At that exact moment, Viktor was sitting in the backyard of his childhood home. He sat with his mom and dad and cried like a little baby. Tears of sadness and rage, and anger, and disappointment. He cried because he no longer had the strength to live his own life. He could no longer work, take care of Jana, and be surrounded by

---

36   Currency of Croatia (HRK)

37   A traditional flatbread

38   A grilled dish of minced meat found traditionally in the Balkan countries, served in groups of five to ten pieces on a plate or in a flatbread

depression, screaming, arguing, and nervous outbursts every day. There was no longer a time of day when he felt positive or relaxed, even just for a few minutes.

Viktor expressed all of these feelings to his parents. How angry he was at Nora and how he was out of excuses for her behavior. He finally said all those words he had been keeping to himself, and which he had been ashamed of, out loud. And then he told them the thing that scared him the most. He did not know how to love her anymore.

14

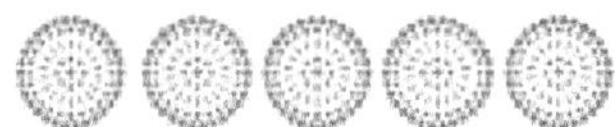

- That is your family, Viktor, and it's your responsibility to take care of them. Nora's depression can't last forever. You have a small child to raise. You know that we can help you with anything whenever you need us, but it is up to you to get your family under control – Vesna was talking as Viktor poured another glass. Her relentless character, in combination with traditional parenting, left little room for emotion. She has always believed that in a family, everybody had their role, and found it very important not to deviate from them. Viktor grew up in such an environment, so he was well aware of her stance on that. On the one hand, his mum was just trying to help him. She was really going out of her way; Viktor could not even imagine what would have happened if it had not been for her help in the last few months. But, despite that, she could not understand what he was really going through. He could not just quench his feelings and perform the role he was supposed to, according to her.

On the other side, there was his dad. Although he tried to look at the situation from Viktor's point of view, the thing he had trouble understanding was why Viktor's work had to suffer. He was always proud of Viktor and his ambition to advance in his career. He knew that Viktor loved working with him, so why did he let his results get so miserable? Why did he not use his job as an escape from everything that was happening at home?

- You have no control over what's happening at home while you're at work anyway. Why don't you at least take that time to relax and devote yourself to what we do.

Viktor no longer had the energy to explain. They had been through the same thing a hundred times. He tried to explain to them what his typical day was like. He tried to explain that he was exhausted, falling apart even. He was done explaining.

- Do you even know what it's like to live with someone who loathes you? I no longer have the need to defend her, dad. Can you imagine yourself not giving a damn if somebody harmed mom? Mom, can you imagine the feeling if you were being hurt and dad was not reacting at all? Nora is no longer the girl I fell in love with. I wanted to keep that girl by my side all my life. Only her. I didn't care if the whole world was against me as long as I was confident that she would stand by me. That girl would not be able to speak the words Nora does now, day after day. It's torture. Hearing those words and seeing her despise me, it hurt beyond measure. But then, it started to make me angry, because I wasn't doing anything. Get it?!? What did I do to deserve this? – Viktor said and threw his glass into the wall. No one reacted, as Viktor seemed to expect. He sat down, poured himself another drink, and turned toward the house. Vesna was already on her way to Jana's room.

- And now? Now, it's the worst part because I stopped caring altogether.

- Son, you have to sort this out with Nora. And with yourself. What you're doing will not help – Mate pointed to Viktor's glass. Mate did not want to see his child suffer so much. He and Vesna were aware of the situation, they knew it was difficult, but they had never seen their son so broken. Mate went to bed, and along the way, he took Viktor's company car keys and put them somewhere where Viktor would not look. In the morning, they had coffee together, and Viktor apologized. It was a weird kind of apology because he was not sorry about telling them anything, he had to tell someone, but he was sorry for making them worry. He took Jana and went home. Nora walked into the apartment half an hour later.

- Hi – she said, coming in with two large bags. Viktor was so surprised that she greeted him that a smile automatically appeared on his face. If he was someone on the outside looking in, he would have realized how sad that really was. How desperate you must be to rejoice at the fact your own wife has spoken to you. Maybe this trip was good for her, he thought, and took the bags so she could get into the apartment. She kissed Jana and sat on the bed in the living room.

- What did you bring? How are you? – Viktor tried cautiously.

- I tried not to take too much, so I only took the things that brought back the fondest memories – Nora answered him, not taking her eyes off sleeping Jana. *Maybe she was really doing better*, Viktor finally dared to think. He went to work and got through a big chunk of his backlog. For a moment, it seemed as these few months of living hell had not even happened. When he got back home, the girls were already asleep, making him realize how late it actually was. He caught himself thinking where he should sleep, but then he scolded himself - he was not going to live like that. It was not normal to have to ponder whether you should or should not lie down next to your own wife. Viktor fell asleep next to Nora, hoping everything would fall into place soon. The bed was empty when he woke up in the morning. *Maybe Nora is already up* - a thought that gave him hope things were looking up. So much time spent in silence and just observing Nora's behavior gave him the ability to automatically notice even the slightest change. But he could also differentiate those small changes by whether they would lead to something positive or to an even bigger downward spiral of depression. He got dressed and headed to the kitchen. Seeing Nora sleeping in the living room felt like a punch in the gut. How could he even think for a second everything would get better just because they had exchanged two sentences the day before? He was such a fool that he felt sorry for himself. Their relationship had not miraculously improved; Nora was already sleeping when he lay beside her. She must have moved to the living room as soon as she felt him there. Viktor got ready and left the apartment angry, sad, and disappointed.

Nora woke up in an empty apartment and, for a moment, did not know where she was. Why was she in the living room, and how did she end up there? Then, she remembered the awful dream that had awakened her. She was tossing and turning, not being able to fall back asleep. When she felt Viktor breathing deeply, she was glad he lay down beside her. Each day he was proving how much love he had for her, and Nora felt terrible for not seeing that in the moments she had been the worst to him. He and Jana were the only things she had left in this world; she knew she had to get her act together. Although being aware of that even at those worst moments, something inside was tearing her apart over and over again, making her go crazy. She had become a depressed and hysterical person that no one can deal with. In those situations, she wanted to slap herself, but instead, she would lash out on everybody else, resenting her own behavior and emotions. It was an endless cycle from which she did not know how to get out of, but if anybody tried to help her, she would feel miserable and weak. She could not stand feeling that way, and consequently, her reaction would always provoke another fight. She was convinced she would be better off if everyone got away from her. And, unquestionably, *they* would be better off. Nora did not want to wake Viktor up, so she moved to the living room. She kissed him gently on the head, catching a whiff of his hair. A scent she barely remembered. It was almost dawn when she fell asleep after watching some stupid movie. But at least it was a dreamless sleep. No dreams were waking her up and keeping her awake, at last.

Viktor was already gone, and for the first time in a long time, Nora wished she had seen him before he left. At that moment, she knew everything was going to be okay. Old Nora was still somewhere inside, and now it was her job to make her come out. She was sick of this shell of a person she had turned into. Even though she had made that decision many times before, her head would always get the best of her. This time it was Nora's time to win. She had to trick her own head by convincing herself she was doing better until she really was. Nora sat down at her laptop and decided to make lunch. Something new, something she had never made before, and following a recipe to the letter. Following a recipe is a crucial thing. If a person who, unlike her, knew how to cook, decided to use half a cup of flour, then she should use that much, not a little bit more just because it did not look right to her. She had been cooking for two hours and could not wait for everything to be ready. For the first time in a long time, she was nervous about Viktor coming home. She hoped he would like it. It was going to be difficult to talk to him and to try and restore their old relationship back, but she hoped that at least he would see that she was really trying and that she still cared.

It has been over an hour and a half since the end of Viktor's workday, and Nora was starting to get really hungry. She wanted to wait for him so they could have lunch together, but she was starving. Also, she could not know how much longer it would take him to get home, so she ate. She put the rest in the oven to wait for him and decided to go for a walk around the building with Jana. From now on, everything was going to be different. She could feel it. She was going to be okay; until she can find a way to deal with everything, she would pretend to be okay. No one around her needed to know what she was going through until she found a way to solve a problem in her head. Jana was sleeping in her stroller. She loved walks; no matter if it was scorching hot or freezing cold outside, that kid loved the fresh air. Jana was the most important person in Nora's life, and Nora was always aware of that. But then she remembered herself in the last couple of months. Nora tried to imagine herself lying in that dark room, or standing in the bathroom with a fistful of pills in her hand, or walking around the house like a zombie. The constant eerie silence, and Nora and Viktor acting like two enemies forced to live together. *Is that the kind of life you decided to create for your daughter? Is that the type of mother you choose to be? Is that what your mother taught you?*

Nora instantly felt ashamed. She could feel her mind starting to drift back to that place from which she cannot snap out of for days on end. She was trying to pull herself together and breathe when something wonderful happened. Jana smiled in her sleep. That was all Nora needed. The one thing she had to learn was how to hold on to those little things, to which her head can respond with gratitude. She just had to be grateful and her mood will improve. It was impossible to be grateful and feel bad at the same time.

Viktor returned to an empty apartment. He was relieved, then immediately saddened for looking forward to coming to an empty apartment. He found an empty, dirty plate in the kitchen and added that to the pile of things that hurt him daily. The fact that Nora prepared the meal only for herself as if he did not exist would usually not bother him at all. But now, everything she would do seemed to bother him. By now, he had also gotten to know his head, emotions, and reactions, so he could recognize some critical moments. This was one of them. Who would have known? Of all the things that had happened in the last several months, one dirty plate was crucial. As soon as that thought went through his head, he just had to laugh. He felt a sudden sense of peace and certainty that everything would be all right. Grateful for that peace of mind, his body immediately relaxed as well. Everything would finally be okay.

Upon entering the apartment, Nora slightly bumped the stroller against the door that did not fully open. Jana budgeted a bit but then continued to sleep as if it did not concern her at all. They came in, and Nora could now see the reason why they got stuck. Two large suitcases, usually stacked on top of their closet, were now blocking their way.

- Nora, we need to talk. Whether you like it or not.

Nora froze in her tracks. She could feel her hands clutching at the stroller, but she could not feel her legs at all. It was this strange combination of adrenaline, hormones, nerves, and everything else that was intended to warn your body in moments like these that something dangerous is about to happen. Something unknown, something that might kill you. She was speechless. But she wanted to speak. With all her heart and soul, she wanted to tell Viktor something, anything, just to stop him from saying something that would ultimately destroy them.

- I don't want to fight. I'm all out of strength.

- What do these suitcases mean?

- I accepted a job in the Netherlands.

- Viktor, please, don't – Nora said so quietly she was not sure if she even said it out loud. She hoped she did, but judging by his cold eyes, she was not convinced.

- I can't live like this anymore.

- Please, don't leave me. I know I'm difficult, and I'm aware of everything I've done to you. I know you've been through hell, but please don't leave me. I can't bear it. I promise you everything will be different. It really will be. I've decided – she sobbed, but Viktor did not seem to notice.

- Oh, really? When did you decide that? Last night, when you left me alone? – his eyes were wide open. For a second, she did not even know what he was talking about. All the little things she did every day that must have been destroying him, how was she not aware of them? And now, it was too late. Seeing his face so closely now, it brought her back to all of the times he would look at her before. The look on his face when she would do something that made him fall in love with her all over again, his eyes when she was sure he loved her, his look when Jana was born, and all the times he was as much hurt by her pain as she was. But the look on his face right now was the worst kind. He was furious.

- I didn't want to wake you, I couldn't sleep. Please, understand me. I'm trying to find a way out of this black hole. You and Jana are all that I have in this world. I'm begging you, don't leave us. I don't know if I could stand it.

- If you could stand it? Nora, we cannot stand each other. Not to mention love and respect. Do you really think we can live like that? This is worse than prison. Everything that could have gone wrong in my life it did.

- Viktor, I beg of you. Just give me one more chance. Please. With all my being, I beg you not to go.

- You are refusing the help you need, so now it's up to you to find it yourself. I can't help you, and if I stay, we'll both go mad. Jana doesn't deserve that. You don't deserve to live like that, and neither do I.

- So, you're telling me you're doing this for us? — Nora's tone changed. She could feel her mood starting to swing in the direction of anger. He had no right to do it this way. Without any warning.

- Viktor, did you really give me a deadline to get over my mom and dad? How can you leave me? — she said softly and calmly, but sending a perfectly clear message.

- How can I leave you? Are you Nora, even aware of what you've been doing? It took us exactly 30 seconds to start fighting. Are you aware that this is all Jana has been listening to for months? I believe this is best for all of us. She'll stay with my parents for a while because...

- That is out of the question, what is wrong with you? — she stopped him immediately. — Jana is my child.

- Well, you haven't exactly been acting like it — mommy! — Viktor said that word with so much disgust that it caught Nora off-guard. She slapped him and automatically covered her mouth, shocked.

They both were. Her reaction was impulsive, and now she was not able to take it back.

- I'm so sorry, I don't know what came over me – Nora tried, but Viktor just stared at her with the blankest look she had ever witnessed. She no longer knew what to do to make him realize what a mistake he was doing. One of those mistakes that could change everything forever.

- Viktor, look at what you're doing. Are you really going to leave your child?

- I'm not leaving my child, you're pushing me away from her!

- Are you out of your mind? You're really going to use that as an excuse, aren't you?

- That's no excuse, Nora, that is my last attempt to preserve my sanity.

- It's the last attempt to save your career! If you are so sure about your decision, then call it as it is.

- You want that? Yes, I'm going to the Netherlands because my career is important to me, and I'm not ashamed of it. Maybe if you had some motivation in your life, you wouldn't spend all your days locked away in a room. I don't plan on abandoning Jana. She will never want for nothing, and I'm not going to stay there forever, but I cannot live with you anymore. Do you understand, Nora? I don't know how to love you anymore. I don't feel a need to make you feel better.

Done. He broke her. What do you even say to something like that? There was no way to make someone love you. And what if there was? Could you really live with the fact you had forced someone to love you? Could you ever really feel loved that way?

Viktor left, and Nora fell to the floor, sobbing, broken, and alone. How did it come to this? How did she end up here? How much more can her heart take? The time was passing as Nora was curled up on the floor, and if she had not heard Jana crying, she might have never gotten back up again. She picked up her daughter and kissed her softly. After wiping the tears off her little face, Nora lay down on the couch with Jana in her arms. She did not want to let her go. Not even for a second, Nora wished to keep on holding the only thing she had in life forever.

15

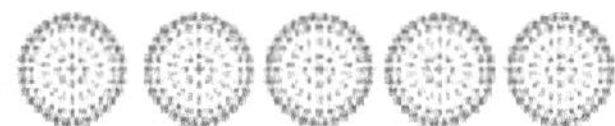

Just how many times in the last few months did she wish for everyone to leave her alone? Well, her wish finally came true. Nora was sitting in her living room, completely left alone. She was incredibly sad, so she tried to differentiate between the sadness she felt when she would lose someone, and the sadness she felt when someone would decide that she had lost them. It was hard to say which one hurt more or less. The first one felt completely unfair, and everyone would wonder what did they do to deserve this. At that moment, people would allow themselves to think that something they had done, good or bad, possibly had an impact on what happened. It was incredibly hurtful and hard to accept, as it would happen unexpectedly, like a slap on the face you did not see coming. And no matter how many times you got slapped, you were always just as shocked and shaken to your core.

But when you would lose someone because they left, that was a choice. It was a result of a series of situations you really could have done something about, but you had not. Or you had, and then you lost them. That is, if you had done nothing, you would possibly still have them. When you would lose someone unexpectedly, you could live the rest of your life believing that they had never intended to leave you. But when someone decided to leave you, you had to live with the fact that someone had made a decision to leave you behind. As if you have never even existed.

Nora felt hurt and ashamed at the same time. Regardless of what she wanted to be the truth, she was aware of her behavior and that it made Viktor leave her. As it would usually happen after overthinking one and the same thing, her thoughts began to drift in different directions. So she quickly drifted from being hurt to being angry. Maybe that was the way she unconsciously shielded herself. If you turned things around for long enough, you would be able to find justification for anything you did in any situation ever.

- What exactly is wrong with him? He abandoned his own child! You don't do that! It's hard, no one ever said it won't be, but that doesn't give you the right to just leave. Technically, you have that right, you're not forced to live with anybody, but you don't just go to another country and leave everything behind. And then what!?! Things are no longer dandy here, so you're just going to make a new life there – Nora was standing in the kitchen washing dishes. She was furious, and that was her way to get everything out of her system. The plates were impeccably scrubbed. She tried to lay down several times, or sit on the couch and watch some TV, but nothing helped, except standing and walking around. Maybe she wanted to walk all of that anger out.

- How could he leave me? – she said out loud and felt a tear slide down her cheek. She could not believe he was really gone. She could not believe she was begging him to stay, and that he was so out of love with her that it meant absolutely nothing to him. One glance at the oven reminded her of the lunch she made. Today was supposed to turn out differently. Today was supposed to be the day when he would see that she decided to get better. She did not mean to tell him that because it sounded stupid: *Viktor, hey, listen, I've decided I'd be better.* She did not want to say that to him because she could imagine what his answers would be like, something in the sense of:

Well, it took you long enough. She was scared of the things he could say to her that would hurt or annoy her. That always turned their discussions into fights, so she decided to show him, instead of telling him. That stupid lunch was supposed to be a clear sign.

And then there was a moment when a new emotion emerged. Anger and sadness were slowly replaced by fear.

Exactly 678 thoughts went through her head in just one minute, and Nora realized just how many reasons for fear she actually had. She and Jana were completely alone in the world. Not only that, they were alone in Viktor's world, and Viktor had just left them. She had nothing. They lived in his apartment, where for the first time, she felt like a stranger. She had no job and had nowhere to run if anything went wrong. What if she was not able to take care of her own child? That feeling was hard to define, but it was one of the worst Nora had ever had. Fear and shame that her daughter would miss something because she is not capable enough. Suddenly Nora's phone was on her ear, and she could hear it ringing, but no one was answering. She realized she had called Monika without even thinking about it. That was probably the only way she could have done that, considering how their last conversation had gone. If Nora had thought about it for just a second before making that call, she would have realized how stupid it was to expect she still had the right to call Monika any time of the day or night. Or the right to call her at all. Nora had lost that right when she intentionally uttered the words she knew would hurt Monika. And she knew how much it would hurt her if Monika did the same to her. And Monika could; she knew her deepest fears, insecurities, and worries. That was what friendship was all about. The privilege of having one of the most potent kinds of relationships in life and the power to completely destroy that person about whom you know every slightest bit. And Nora did precisely that. She knew exactly what Monika was afraid of, and she used it in the ugliest way possible. Remembering that, Nora got so ashamed of her behavior and treatment of Monika that she became physically ill. She ran to the bathroom and vomited. Still sitting on the bathroom floor and leaning against the toilet, Nora cried aloud. Not only was she sad, alone, and forgotten, she was guilty of it all. *You deserve to feel this way, you piece of shit.* She lost just about everything she had ever had in her life. Whether by her own merit or by some higher verdict. If she could have only one wish, she would wish to fall asleep and never wake up again. She did not see any other way out.

At that exact moment, Jana cried out. It sounded like she was having a nightmare. Tears streamed down her small innocent face, and she was terrified. Nora got up and went to her crib. She picked her up gently and hugged her. As if by magic, they both calmed down. The reactions that occur in the human body when you feel close to someone affect the brain at an incredible speed and can relax you in seconds. Isn't it wonderful that a hug is one of the ways to trigger those reactions? Nora could feel that everything would be all right. She would make sure everything was all right. This child was her life, and there was nothing she would not do for her. *Mommy will look after you forever. I promise you, my love.*

Nora decided to sit down and gather her thoughts. Sleep was clearly not an option, so maybe she could try to use that head of hers for something useful. If nothing else, she could determine the problems she was facing. It would not be fun, but it would at least stop her from talking to a wall and to herself. She started with their current situation. Vesna and Mate loved Jana very much, Nora knew that as well as that they would never let anything happen to her. The thing she was not so sure about was her own position in that whole scenario. She remembered Viktor's plan to leave Jana with them, and suddenly she was not scared anymore. *Okay, that's out of the question. My child will not be taken away from me.* But now the panic took over because she had no idea what to do first. She could not breathe, so she went to the balcony to get some air. The night was slowly turning into day, and only then Nora realized she had been up the whole night. All of a sudden, the doorbell rang, and Nora was overwhelmed by a sense of dread, for she had no idea who it might be. The past experiences made her fear it could be something terrible.

She took a deep breath and opened the door. And there she was, that beautiful fool that was Monika, holding yogurt and the peanut puffs. If, at that moment, Nora has not felt the most profound gratitude in her life, she probably never would.

- Yogurt may have gone bad, but that's just because I've been waiting for you to come to your senses for a while.

Nora just started weeping. She felt such an adrenaline rush that she would have probably collapsed if she had not immediately grabbed the wall. She did not deserve Monika. She did not deserve to be cared for by someone she was so cruel to. How beautiful and forgiving person Monika had to be? It was the gesture and the moment when every cell in your body is sure that someone loves you. Truly loves you, like you are a part of them. Those are the feeling the life should consist of, and everyone on Earth certainly has such a person. You just need to find them. Find, appreciate, and never let go of them.

- Nora, for the love of God, stop whining.

She knew everything. Monika knew how sorry Nora was, that she loved her too and would never intentionally hurt her. She also knew that Nora would get better and that it was the best thing for both of them to leave Nora alone until she got out of that state she was in. Of course, that did not mean that those words did not hurt Monika. She was sad and angry at Nora, but all along, she knew it was just a short-term thing. Because, when it came to the people you love, you just knew those things.

- But I treated you like the biggest shit – Nora said through tears.

- That's true, yes. And don't get me wrong, I'm ready to be real' angry at you, but not right now. We have to fix you up a little bit because it makes no sense to be mad at you when you are so broken – Monika said, hugging Nora.

Imagine you are falling apart, and you feel you are just a pile of little broken pieces. You think only the worst about yourself, how you deserve nothing and no one in your life, but you cannot escape from your reality. Then someone comes and hugs you, and all those pieces come together again. And you are whole again. Because of one single genuine hug.

Monika made coffee, and they sat down on the balcony. Nora told her everything that had happened with Viktor. Without a second thought or any restraint, she confessed how sad, angry, and hurt him leaving made her. Nora also acknowledged that she was the one to blame. She said that she is anxious about staying in his apartment because she did not know how Vesna was going to react. Moving to Monika's occurred to both of them, but that was not possible because Monika recently moved to a small studio apartment. Both of them found it strange that Nora, at one point in time, did not know where Monika lived. But they began to talk about everyday things almost immediately as if it has not been two months since they had last seen each other. At that moment, Nora realized what the cure for absolutely every problem in the world was. Coffee with a friend.

They spent an hour and a half on that balcony, going inside only when Jana woke up. Monika ran as if the house was on fire so she could take Jana before Nora did. Nora, on the other hand, walked in slowly, snuggled up on the couch, and peacefully fell asleep.

- You know, Jana, I get that she didn't sleep all night and that she should really sleep right now, but her continually sleeping is really starting to get on my nerve – Monika used that sarcastic tone of voice that was the best proof that everything would be all right.

16

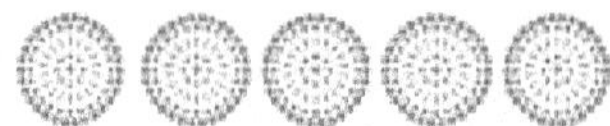

Three days passed since Viktor left. Nora still had her mood swings, but anger was indeed prevailing. Each day without him was getting more and more strange as everything else was going on like usual. Nora and Jana would wake up in the morning, go for a walk, play, cook, and look for jobs for mommy. Nora could not help but feel sad and fearful about him leaving, but every time, it would all come down to the fact that it was his choice.

She heard the doorbell and thought it was probably Monika, confused why she was acting all nice ringing the doorbell. She opened the door and saw Vesna. Awkward. Both were silent and were just looking at each other for a second, a second that seemed a lot longer.

- You mind if I come in?

- No, of course. Excuse me – Nora let her pass.

Vesna walked into the apartment, took off her jacket and her shoes, and immediately sat on the floor beside Jana. She started baby-talking, squeezing her and playing with her, while Nora was not sure where to put herself.

- Maybe for a coffee or juice? – she went for a polite question you ask when you do not know what to say.

- No, thanks. I won't be long.

Vesna just glanced at her briefly and returned to playing with Jana.

Nora was standing in the kitchen, facing away from the living room where the two of them were playing on the floor, and she was holding back the laughter. *Like, we're not going to mention anything? Really? Are we pretending everything is normal? Fine, let's see how that goes.* Nora knew exactly what Vesna would say about a father abandoning his family. She knew her traditional stance about such behavior – you just don't do that, period. Whatever the reason. The only thing Nora was not sure about was whether this also applied if a father in question was her son. *Maybe she doesn't know? Yeah, right, she probably helped him pack.* Soon, Vesna got up and headed for the door. Again, Nora was not sure what to do, so she went after her.

- I just wanted to come and see you both. Take care.

- Of course, thank you for a visit – Nora said with a smile.

- Hell if I know, my daughter, what just happened – she continued quietly as she closed the door.

- Nana.

- Yes, your nana, I know, thanks for the info.

The visits started occurring every other day and were less and less courteous. Nora would offer Vesna coffee every time, but Vesna always refused. Nora expected them to be able to sit down and talk about the whole situation like two adults. But that did not happen, so Nora kept getting out of Vesna's way so she could play with Jana. She had no intention of affecting the relationship between them and Jana. Jana was their granddaughter, and they were her grandparents, forever. She remembered how special it was when her mom and dad were with Jana, and she was grateful for having those memories for the rest of her life.

- Daddy asks about you all the time, honey – Vesna said louder, obviously so that Nora could hear. She did hear, of course, but of all the ways Vesna could have mentioned Viktor, this one took her by surprise. Nora did not know why, but she did not expect it. Nevertheless, she did not react but just continued to peel the potatoes for lunch.

So, they are in touch. Unbelievable. And like Jana would be excited all day about dad asking about her – she's one, for God's sake, she doesn't get it. Why doesn't he call here? What an idiot, both him and that subtle mother of his. In a second, Nora became furious and felt the need to say a lot of things to Vesna, but she held it in. After all, it was not Vesna's fault. Those stupid remarks certainly did not help, but she was not to blame. And besides, Nora did not want Vesna to tell that jerk how crazy Nora had a fit at the mere mention of his name. *Screw that asshole!*

Nora spent her days walking around and playing with Jana. She enjoyed that, but she needed a job. The money was almost gone, and the expenses were just piling up. Monika jumped in as much as she could, but that was not the solution. Nora did not get a single job interview yet. She was beginning to panic, and as much as she tried to calm herself down, she knew she was close to a breaking point. The only thing missing was one of Vesna's remarks. Vesna showed up at the door with diapers and a bunch of food for Jana.

- Look, honey, daddy sent you a toy – she said, sitting down next to Jana on the floor.

She's gotta be kidding me, Nora thought. She was losing her patience. Maybe she should go to the store, or just somewhere outside, before snapping at that woman. But she gave up on that idea; Nora knew that would be the smartest thing to do at this point, but given how much pressure she was already under because of the whole situation, it was as if she was subconsciously looking for an excuse to lash out.

- Nora, Viktor has sent you money to enroll Jana in preschool. Considering you're not paying for the apartment because it's Viktor's, with this amount of money, you can pay for some nicer nursery for Jana.

- She's not going to go to preschool until I find a job. It doesn't make sense for her to go while I'm home alone.

- It certainly doesn't make sense for you to be home, true, but someone needs to take care of her while you're going to the job interviews. You're going to them, right?

- I'll handle it, don't you worry. She will certainly not be left alone in the apartment.

Good, Nora, you were good. You didn't snap, cool, way to go, she told herself, but Vesna continued speaking to Jana, and all of Nora's efforts to control herself went down the drain.

- Your daddy loves you very much, you know that?

- Vesna, would you care to explain to me why you keep telling her that? Do you think she won't know that she has a dad? Do you think I'll hide that from her? Do you think anyone is stopping him from being with his daughter? What exactly are you trying to achieve with this nonsense?

Nora was obviously done holding back.

- You, Nora, can think whatever you want about Viktor, but he left so he could take care of his family.

- Even you don't believe that. Please, don't sell me that story about looking for a better life, because his life was pretty good right here.

- He's taking care of Jana; she will never miss anything. I mean, you have a roof over your head because of him. And Jana will always have one – Vesna said, and left the apartment.

- Did she just casually throw me out of the picture? – Nora asked Jana, who was just turning the toy around in her hands.

At that moment, Nora promised her daughter they would move to their own apartment. She had made her decision and would find a way to make it happen, even if she had to take a leap of faith.

Vesna continued with her stupid remarks, but Nora found the perfect way to deal with them. After each of Vesna's sentences, Nora would immediately think of what she would answer back, then she would just laugh at that response, calm down, and just keep quiet. It was not the best coping mechanism, but to Nora, it was undoubtedly the most entertaining one. Sometimes, it was the only way to survive until Vesna, and all of her hair would leave the apartment.

- I think there is always work for those who want to work.

Of course. I turned down so many offers because I'm waiting for something perfect. There's no way I would take just anything. No, I'm waiting for them to offer me directorship, nothing less will do, and that's that.

- Everyone with a degree, who I know, is working.

Beside me, you know precisely three other people, you crazy woman.

- Viktor is a great father for taking care of Jana.

Well done, Viktor, he should teach some fucking seminar on how to take care of a family.

- Still, no job?

Oh, no, I found a job, but I got bored the first day, so I quit.

- Look, I don't understand, my neighbor just went to a job interview and got the job, and now she's working.

Nora might have found the way to ignore Vesna's incredibly subtle remarks, but nothing helped her with the overwhelming fear and panic that kept growing each day. Every new e-mail in her inbox gave her new hope, but it was always a rejection. She was checking her e-mail every ten minutes, and it slowly turned into an obsession. At that point, there were 34 sent job applications in her sent-mail folder.

- Something has to stick, right, Jana? – Jana spat, and Nora chose to interpret that as *yes, mommy*.

Nora was able to find the will to live through Jana. By now, she could consciously foresee the dark thoughts that had hitherto plunged her into the bed in a darkened room. A desire to provide a healthy life for her daughter was so strong that Nora could no longer imagine giving in to that mindset. She still missed her mom and dad with every fiber of her being, but now she allowed herself to feel that way without feeling guilty. She also missed that idiot Viktor, but her anger towards him made it easier for her to deal with it.

Their mornings would start when Jana decided to wake up. After cuddling in bed, Nora would make them breakfast and coffee for herself. The moment that Jana would get distracted with her toys, Nera would sit down at her laptop and scroll through all the websites and portals with job listings she knew of. She was going through schools, ministries, preschools, the Croatian Employment Service website, and everything else that would come to her mind. Initially, Nora only applied for jobs in her profession. Then she started applying for everything she thought she would know how to do, but now she had to start applying for vocational training without employment positions.

Those kinds of adverts made up, she roughly estimated, 80 percent of all job listings, so even if she got something, it would probably be vocational training.

- Jana, look, I found it. The most realistic job listing ever. They are looking for a person aged 25 or younger with a college degree and a minimum of 5 years of work experience. I mean, that person doesn't exist, unless they enrolled in college at the age of 15, graduated by the age of 20, immediately found a job, and worked there ever since – Nora turned to Jana, who was beaming at her.

She was looking at Nora with that look she knew by now would make her mom laugh. Nora shifted her attention to her gorgeous daughter. Her blonde locks with playful curls, and her eyes as blue as the sky, were all Nora needed for happiness. She already admired the person her daughter would grow into. Playful and eager to explore everything, Jana would spend hours examining the same toy. She was funny and lively; she was smart – she absorbed everything to the point that Nora had to be careful about what she said in front of her. She was Nora's best friend and gave her life meaning and purpose.

Nora's mild panic attacks were getting more frequent. It has been three weeks now, and she did not even get an interview. She tried to write a special application letter for each application because she believed that made a difference, but slowly she was losing all hope. She did her usual ad search again this morning, but there were no new listings, so she decided to go for a walk with Jana and see if there was any news at the Croatian Employment Service. She turned around just as Jana stood up and kept standing. Nora jumped so fast, she nearly spilled a full cup of hot coffee all over herself. Jana did not react to any of that, as she entirely concentrated on making that first step. At that moment, Nora jumped half-way across the room, screaming with excitement and grabbing her phone to record it.

Jana took two steps and fell down, then started laughing

because Nora looked like a lunatic you had to laugh at. She was screaming *"good job!",* laughing and jumping around Jana, who did not understand anything except that they were being happy.

The same day Vesna visited again, and this time Nora was happy about it because she had to inform as many people as possible about her daughter's incredible accomplishment.

- Let's show grandma what you can do – Nora was excited like a little kid. She lifted Jana on her feet and waited for her to take another step. Jana wobbled for a bit and eventually made one small step. It was the most elegant tentative step Nora had ever seen, so she started screaming, laughing, and clapping again. Vesna joined that excitement, which made Jana laugh even more.

- I'm just sad your dad's not here to see this – Vesna said in that tragic tone that was really starting to get on Nora's nerves.

- You know what, Vesna? Viktor chose not to be here for this – Nora realized how painful it was when someone saddens you in such a joyful moment. She really hoped to share these moments with Vesna, no matter the situation. Why did Vesna hate her so much? Could she not at least acknowledge the fact that it was Nora and her son who created that little miracle of a child, who Vesna undoubtedly adored? Was that not reason enough for her to be at least somewhat nice to Nora?

- It wasn't exactly a choice if his back was against the wall, and you know it.

Nora was immediately ashamed and scared that this negative feeling would break her again. He left because Nora was impossible. There was a lump in her throat, indicating that her next word would be uttered through tears, so she just stayed silent. It did not matter what the word was or to whom it was addressed; the moment that stupid anxiety came around, you just knew you would start to cry if you did not shut up and calm down. The only thing that Nora wanted to tell Vesna was that she had already sent Viktor a video of Jana walking, because she had never doubted his love for Jana, nor would she want him to miss anything in Jana's life, even if two of them would never work things out. But she did not. Vesna soon left, as usual, leaving Nora judging herself for everything that had ever gone wrong.

After lunch, Jana sat on the couch, holding a remote control. She looked at Nora with sleepy eyes and said: *"Catoons."*

- Yes, cartoons, a great idea.

Jana fell asleep within three minutes, curled up in Nora's embrace, and everything was calm and peaceful again. Nora was looking at her beautiful child and felt grateful to have her in her life. The image of her mom and dad came back to her mind; she could exactly imagine just how much her dad would jump from happiness if he could see Jana's first steps. Her mom would probably make a cake with shoes on top because everything important had to be celebrated with a cake. Nora could see it all clearly in her head, even though she had never seen them in such a situation. This feeling of sadness for her parents would never go away, but that was okay. They deserved to never be forgotten.

A tear rolled down her face, but Nora had a good feeling. Still looking at her child, she knew she must be the kind of parent her parents were to her. They were the best role model she could have wished for, and because of that, she knew exactly what to do in every possible situation. Now her mission was to find a job. She was the one who had to provide security for both of them. There was no way she would allow for them to be dependent on Viktor or his parents, and let them in any way speak for Jana. She would go from door to door until someone agrees to hire her, and that was it.

As if she remembered she had fallen asleep without her song, Jana began to squirm. Nora started a rhyme they recited every time before bed, and Jana joined in with her attempts at shaping the words she had learned so far.

- There is one beautiful little...

- *... girl...,*

- ... and her mommy loves her the most in this...

- *... world.*

- She makes her mommy feel very...

- *... blessed...*

- ...and in the whole world, that feeling is the...

- *... best.*

- If mommy could wish for only one...

- *...thing...*

- ...it would be for her baby to have...

- *...ewything.*

17

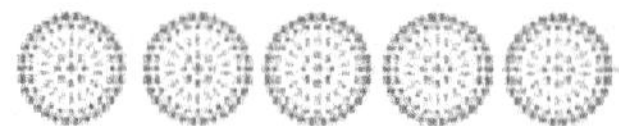

She saw the notification for a new e-mail on her phone and hurried to the computer. For some strange reason, she preferred to sit in front of the screen to check her messages. Maybe she was just using that time to prepare in case the news was not good, or it was just a lot harder to press or send something by accident over a computer than a cell phone. The e-mail was from a school she had gone to for an interview for a vocational training position, and now they were letting her know that somebody else had gotten the spot. It was not the first time she had been rejected, and as it seemed, it was not going to be the last, but this time it was particularly painful. She sat in front of the screen and cried, both with sadness and anger. *How is it even possible that I didn't meet the criteria at any interview? What the hell is wrong with me?!?*

Maybe something really was wrong. This could not be true. How was a person even supposed to handle so many rejections? Perhaps she was not even eligible for that stupid training program? It was 6 in the morning when Nora decided to research everything she could about the vocational training without employment. She had to find some reason; otherwise, she would start attacking the people who interviewed her to tell her exactly why she did not get the job.

- So, the program is designed for people under 29 years of age. Which I am, okay. The person must be registered with the Employment Service for at least 30 days, which I certainly am. And they must have less than a year of work experience, which I have, that is, don't have thanks to all of you who don't want to hire me. Thank you from the bottom of my heart.

Nora knew a lot about the program, but she never really explored all the elements of it and the way it was conceived. The more she read about it on the Internet, the angrier she would become. After a while, she realized that she was actually looking for some piece of text that would say how all of this information was not true because there was no freaking way there was a country that allowed for this nonsense to pass through. Monika, who came over for coffee and to play with Jana, arrived at just the right time for Nora to take out her frustrations on her.

- Monika! Did you know that a person doing vocational training is listed as unemployed? I mean, why is that? How is it possible to work 40 hours a week and still be listed as an unemployed person? Tell me, how's that normal?

- Of course, it's not normal, I just don't understand why you are so shocked. The fact that this program has even gone through and is being carried out tells you enough.

- But it's so stupid! And what's the deal with that not being a part of your occupational record? I mean, you're there like everyone else, right?

- I don't know, Nora, I haven't looked that much into it.

- I have, don't you worry. It was even more ridiculous at the beginning. I mean, it's already unbelievable that the program was even suggested, but then for enough people to read that and say – *oh, what a great idea* – preposterous! Initially, when the program was introduced in 2010, it was for people who had to pass professional state or mastership exam by the age of 25 for high school or 29 for college level, and those persons had to have less than 6 months of work experience. Then in 2012, they changed their minds and included the people who did not have to pass those exams but had less than 6 months of experience and have been registered with the Service for at least 90 days. Like in the sense of, *great, guys, you have been looking for a job for three months now, and you are finally qualified to be an unemployed person for a salary of 1,600 kuna.* Hey, 1,600 kuna! To be clear, that's pocket money. And then, that same year, they realized that those 90 days were a stupid idea, so they agreed on having 30 days at the Service and less than a year of work experience.

- I mean, it's obvious how much they evaluated the program before its implementation when they altered the basic conditions every other month.

- Exactly, but that wasn't the end of it. Transportation expenses were paid according to how and how far you were traveling every day, but only up to 1,000 kuna. As if it's ludicrous that you could need more than that every month. And then, the big turnaround of 2015! The figure od 1,600 kuna, as it seemed, was really low; if you think about it, that's not right! So they decided to make it 2,400 kuna.

- Outstanding! Do you have any idea what you can do with 2,400 kuna?!? Especially if you live with your parents, you don't have to pay for anything and, I don't know, get a job across the street from your house. And let's be real, it's everyone's dream to live with their parents forever. In that case, you can live like a king with 2,400 kuna. You can eat whatever you want. I don't get it, Nora, where is the problem? – Monika said sarcastically.

- Yeah, maybe I am overreacting a bit. And I think they suspected that because they canceled paid sick leave this last March. So, if you don't come to work one day, they will deduct, let's say, 109 kuna and your travel expenses for that day. I'm serious, they cut, like, 7 kuna off for travel expenses, because a poor, unemployed fool like you didn't come to work that one day. Because, when you come to buy a monthly train ticket, you can for sure tell them: *Ma'am, can you give me a monthly ticket but not for the whole month, but for 27 days since it's flu season, so if you could charge me less because I will probably be sick some of those days.*

- I saw something on Facebook today, some new idea to cut off transportation expenses if you are traveling by car. I mean, it's obvious why. Cars run on air.

- It's disgusting, really. I feel like they took my diploma, a symbol of those damned 5 years of studying, exams, classes, nerves, and money, and just pissed all over it.

- That's what it seems like, yes, but I think their answer to that would be that it's not the only way to have a job. I mean, they justify it as a program that should encourage employment, not by being the only option.

- I understand that, but they didn't subject employers to any conditions, so nobody wants to hire a person on a normal contract when this allows them to get an educated person who will be entirely paid by the Government.

- I think employers are required to keep at least some people if they want to keep using the vocational training next year.

- That is true, but I'm not sure that anyone is actually looking into that and checking if they really do it. Also, that is a requirement for those employers who are taking in three or more people for the training. For example, if you hired three persons for the vocational training, you have to keep at least one of them. You know how many of them only look for one person for the vocational? Most of them. And for them, that's not a requirement.

Monika fully sympathized with Nora. She did not have it easy, looking for a job, with a child to worry about, all alone. There were no parents to step in financially, and she had nothing of her own, so if they decided to kick her out of the apartment, she had nowhere to go. Nora had nothing, but every day she had to create all that she and Jana needed. In a country that encouraged childbirth and starting a family, a mother with a university-level education who was living alone with her child had to hope to get a vocational training position, paid only 2,400 kuna. An amount that could barely cover monthly food costs for two people.

The vocational training program angered and aggravated every young person who graduated, either from high school or college, and entered the labor market, but especially someone who was in Nora's situation and had no other option.

- I tried to figure out a way how to cover everything we need with those 2,400 kuna, and there is no way, Monika. I can't even find an apartment for the two of us, even a room, for less than 500 kuna, plus let's say 300 kuna for utility bills, and then there are diapers, food, and everything else I need for Jana. I'm left with around 400 kuna for the whole month, and I still didn't eat anything or pay for the trip to that, let's call it a job, or for example, Jana's preschool.

- Yes, but Nora, Viktor should pay for something too.

- He does. That is, he sends money for Jana, but that's not the point. The point is that, even with a diploma, I can't provide myself and my child a roof over our heads, but I have to depend on him and his parents, who can kick me out of this apartment whenever they feel like it.

Nora was scared, but it was not that familiar fear when you panic about something and then calm down. This was a constant feeling of helplessness because there was nothing to do but wait. Her days were too long. Not having enough money was making her more and more anxious, but she did not feel comfortable sharing that with anybody. Every time the bills would arrive, she would feel nauseous and have stomach cramps. The restless feeling would also come about every time she picked up the last diaper or used up anything in the apartment. Her savings account was getting dangerously close to zero, and her fear was growing day by day. She had to force herself to eat as she completely lost her appetite, and to have a good night's sleep was a concept she had forgotten all about.

She was aware that, unfortunately, she was not alone in this. Most of her peers were dealing with this job search problem, and the situation was alarming. Although this topic was regularly mentioned all over the media, Nora had a feeling that no one really talked about it. The news was filled with those well-known phrases and slogans that politicians use to try to show they cared, but Nora saw right through that fake compassion. She wondered if any of them could look her in the eye and say that this was a worthwhile program. Or any of so many young people who moved abroad because they could not find work here. Of course, people were leaving for all sorts of different reasons, but there were so many of them who actually wanted to stay here and use their knowledge and skills to build a life and start a family.

What made her even more disheartened was the fact that people were getting used to it. Until her current situation, she had never known or been bothered about unemployment in the country. She did feel sorry whenever she would hear some isolated story about a person having a hard time finding a job, but as hard as it was for her to admit it now, she had never thought about it for longer than that one moment. She felt terrible, of course, for all the people who could not find work, but that was not her problem at the time. It was scary to think that now the whole society could start feeling a similar way – you feel bad, but you have heard about the lousy unemployment rate so often that you get used to it. You get used to the fact that such time has come and that there is not much that can be done about it.

Although the whole situation with Viktor and Vesna was pretty dumb, Nora was grateful for everything Vesna was bringing her, even though she felt terribly pitiful that she had to depend on it. Monika offered her help as much as she could, but she had prolonged her studies and was still working student jobs. Nora was trying to stay positive, but it was becoming increasingly difficult to believe that everything would be all right.

- Janaaaa! They invited me for an interview! – Jana was merely grinning as Nora jumped around her.

They began their usual routine. Nora threw everything she owned from the closet around the apartment as she was searching for the perfect combination to wear for the interview. At the same time, she called Monika to see if she could watch Jana, who was already playing with her mom's clothes. Nora was excited and nervous before every interview; she had the jitters which she tried not to show, but that made her even more nervous. But as nervous as she was, at least something was happening. The interview went well, or as Nora later explained to Monika – *I'm sure I came across like a fool at least 4 times, but overall I have a good feeling about it*. And then came the hard part – the wait. Nora did not know what was worse; waiting for someone to respond to her application, or waiting for the feedback from an interview. In fact, she generally hated stupid waiting.

And just to make the wait a bit more bearable for Nora, Jana decided she was not having a good day. She was in a bad mood, crying all the time – she did not want to play, she was tired, and she did not want to sleep. There were occasionally these days when there was no chance for her to calm down, and Nora sometimes really believed that her child had decided to have a day like that. That was the only explanation, as she did not believe in demons and exorcisms.

- Will you sleep?

- I won't!

- Well, that's too bad, you still have to.

They stared at each other like they were competing who would last longer.

- Jana, you can pout all you want, but you will have to do it lying down. Let's go to bed.

- I won't – she said quietly and went to bed.

- Well, you may not understand how pouting works, but it seems to me that this whole "I won't" thing is not so clear to you either.

It took Jana an hour and a half to fall asleep, and when she finally did, Nora sat at her computer. She got a reply. Another rejection letter. Quietly, she started crying. She could feel all those heavy emotions beginning to weigh her down. She poured herself a glass of wine and sat down on the balcony. There was no more strength in her. She tried to fool her head with positive thoughts, but it was all pointless. Sad and scared, she felt utterly alone, without anyone or anything to turn to.

The doorbell jolted her from her thought and Jana from sleep. *Great*, she thought, *she slept for barely half an hour, which means that her super-mood will only continue.*

- Good afternoon.

- Hello, Vesna – *the last thing I need right now* - come on in.

Vesna immediately went in Jana's direction, who was already sitting in the living room, still sleepily holding her doll. Nora just proceeded to the kitchen and began preparing the food for lunch. She offered Vesna coffee or juice as usual, which Vesna regularly declined. Nora reminded herself to pay more attention to Vesna's responses because she just might surprise her one day with a "yes" that Nora would unintentionally disregard.

- You and your mom hang out all day long, huh, honey? It's so nice you have that privilege – Vesna said that in a baby voice, which made it even worse since the message was obviously for Nora and not endearing at all. *Please, God, let this be her last comment because I will throw a ladle at her. And I'm afraid I won't be sorry if it hit her.*

- How's the job search going?

- Not so good, I guess I haven't had any luck yet – Nora said unwillingly because of all the days she did not want to talk about it, today was the worst one.

- Unbelievable.

Calm down, Nora.

- Viktor is still sending money for Jana, so I bought her some things.

- Great.

- Great for you, yes.

- Yes, Vesna, I feel just great.

- You have to take responsibility for your actions. This pity party for Nora has to stop. Let's be real, you were impossible. I'm not saying it's easy to find a job, but I don't think it's impossible.

Nora silently cried. She stood in the kitchen, waiting for Vesna to leave because she had no strength to argue with her. She felt miserable, worthless like a piece of trash. Incompetent, alone, and attacked. She just waited for Vesna to say that it would be better for Jana to stay with them or Viktor. What if eventually, that turned into truth? Vesna did not stay much longer because Jana got irritable again and was in no mood to play. Nora asked Monika to come and watch Jana in the morning if she could.

The next morning she was ready as soon as Monika arrived. They quickly drank coffee, then Nora hurried to the coffee bar she worked at as a student to beg for a job. She knew that the boss would be there in the morning, and she hoped he could help her. The fact that he had always been pleased with her work made her hopeful he would take her back. She walked into the bar that she knew like the back of her hand. The atmosphere was dimmed and calm, as it was early in the morning. Only a few regular guests were sitting at their tables and drank their morning coffee. Nothing has changed since she was last here. The walls were still decorated with classic movie posters, which Nora always liked to look at, as they seemed so valuable being so large and framed.

Boss Mirko was standing behind a long counter facing the entrance, while nine small round tables were still in the back of the bar. Mirko was a man in his forties, who decided to open a coffee bar because he had the opportunity to get a locale for a bargain. Now, given how much the situation has changed, he had to work his own shifts to break even at the end of the month. He was a good man, and if he could, Mirko would surely have helped Nora, but as he explained to her, he was not in a position to pay anyone at the moment. He wished things were different, for both of their sakes, but at the moment he could only promise her that he would let her know immediately if he heard about any openings. Nora thanked him and, knocked down again, headed home completely broken-spirited.

18

They started another day with a morning coffee on the balcony while Jana was playing around them. She was now steady on her feet, which meant she could reach more things, and Nora could no longer take her eyes off her. It was time to thoroughly tidy up that small balcony, as Nora always had to take the junk out of Jana's hands, stuff that she did not even know where there or how Jana found it. Monika was trying to fix Jana's ponytail, but her fluffy blond hair just skipped to a pot with a flower that had done its time on this earth a long time ago.

- I have to register with the Service, what's that process like? – Monika asked as she was taking one of the mugs Nora had carried from the kitchen.

- It's dumb, but, well, you have to register. You go there with all the papers and get your advisor; I got some chick Darija. She seems fine, but, like, I wouldn't really say she loves the job she does. Basically, you're entitled to a meeting where you talk about you. The advisor writes down everything about your education, work experience, and job preferences. She asked me if I would agree to do jobs that are not in my field and which require only high-school education, and I said no. She looked at me exactly the same way Vesna looks at me, as in – *look at her, she would like to pick and choose*. Actually, I was only curious about her reaction, so I corrected myself and said that I would do anything, but that I would appreciate it if they would try to find me a job in my profession. She said that's fine and then went on to explain the ordinance for some time – Nora spoke while her eyes looked for suspiciously quiet Jana. She found her by the flower, taking out the soil out of the pot.

- Ordinance on what? On how to get to the employment office? – Monika laughed.

- That's right, it's called the Ordinance on Active Job Search and Availability for Work. I'm not making this up, it really does exist.

- Thank God, imagine if we did not have that written down. Where would we end up?

- Right, right. Everything you need to do to be an eligible unemployed person, it's all there. Serious business, not simple at all. It made me laugh a lot when I was there, so I had to research it later.

- Of course, you did. You and probably no one else ever.

- Probably true, but in any case, there are some programs there, even 9 of them. For example, you have that first meeting, then individual consultations, then group consultations, and some workshops, and then, listen to this one – *defining and implementing the activities and objectives of the Job Integration Agreement*. Because I mean, how will you find a job if you don't understand that agreement, just how?

- Oh, come on, you're lying. So that means that, since you still don't have a job, you didn't go to any of that yet?

- Oh, no, no. I did as I was told because otherwise, I would get unregistered.

- Okay, so they have a general idea of what the process should look like. And according to that, I should go there every so often for a few hours so we can find me a job together. But what does it actually look like?

- You really only have to send an e-mail every month. You write down everything you've done regarding your unemployment. For example, the jobs you applied for and stuff like that. Actually, I should go there and ask them about all those workshops' dates, but I think they would tell me to stop being silly – Nora remarked, and they both laughed. Whether that was funny or sad was less important.

- And so, I send them an e-mail every month in which I list all the jobs I applied to and say that nothing has happened yet. And every month that lady replies to me: *Dear Nora, I have recorded your monthly check-in. Keep on checking listings and sending applications; I hope you will soon get an invitation for some testing or another interview.* And that's that. We have a profound relationship going on.

- I need to register quickly then, so that I can have that kind of support, too – Monika laughed, as she had no other comment on a system functioning this way.

- Yes, for sure. I haven't yet received any proposal for a listing I should apply for from them, but I know there is a limited number of times you can turn them down. So, I'm actually glad they didn't send me anything yet, at least until they send me something worthwhile.

- Why?

- I read on some forum that a girl got a proposal to apply for some position in, I don't know, Rijeka, and she lives in Zagreb. And she is not allowed to reject it, but in Rijeka, she doesn't have a place to stay. Imagine if they send me such a proposal for, let's say, Zagreb. I got no one there; with the vocational wage, there is no way I can afford an apartment and living costs and preschool, nor can I cover a daily trip from Osijek to Zagreb. And considering that it would probably cost more than 1,000 kuna, neither can they cover it for me. But then, if I reject it, I am automatically unregistered from the

Service and no longer qualified to apply for vocational training.

- Horrible – Monika commented on her way to the kitchen.

- Nora, I think you got a message or something, your phone's buzzing.

- Probably an e-mail in which they tell me how they had decided on someone else, but that they wish me the best of luck – Nora said in a tone as if she was joking, but actually, she did not find it funny at all. She opened an e-mail on her phone and carelessly scanned the message. The moment she started putting her phone down, she realized something seemed strange. She ran to the computer and waited for the screen to turn on. After refreshing her inbox, she opened the last message. She made it! They picked her!

- Monikaaaa! I got the job! – she screamed so loudly that Monika and Jana got scared.

- Really?!?! Finally! – Monika jumped and gave her friend a long bear hug. Jana twirled around them in confusion until Nora took her into her hands and started kissing her. Monika played some music, and they just jumped, screamed, and laughed. At one point, Nora stopped, looked at Monika and Jana goofing around, and smiled. She could not remember the last time she felt this good. She was not sure which position it actually was because she had sent so many applications and gone to so many interviews that everything got mixed up, but right now, it did not really matter. Everything was going to be okay. Things would finally be set in motion. At last. Once again, they turned Nora's closet inside out in search of the perfect combination for the meeting tomorrow, and after only two hours of the fashion police session, everything was ready. That night Nora fell asleep next to her daughter with a smile on her face and a sense of immense gratitude.

She arrived at the school half an hour early, just in case. Monika again rearranged her schedule so she could jump in and watch Jana. Nora decided she would prepare dinner for Monika with all of her favorite food. She walked around so nobody inside the building would see her standing in front of it for half an hour. Like an idiot who could not tell time. *Yes, Nora, because when you walk in circles, that makes you seem completely normal.*

The building was tall and a bit frightening. The yellow façade could use a renovation, as it was damaged and already repaired in several places. At the front, between the three windows, there were imitation pillars colored in shades of yellow. Nora tried to imagine how powerful the building must have looked when it was brand new. White ornaments were carved around the windows and on the walls between the two floors, suggesting that the building was quite old. Contemporary buildings tend to be dull and simple because nowadays everything was considered too tacky. This building had large, tall windows symmetrically arranged to allow as much natural light in as possible. The longer Nora looked at it, the more she could imagine herself coming to work here every day. She looked at her watch and decided that arriving ten minutes early could be interpreted as a good sign, so her little walk around the school was over. At the entrance, they escorted her to the principal's office on the second floor. She stood at the door for a few seconds, took a deep breath, and knocked.

The principal's office did not look like she had imagined, given the exterior of the building. The level of natural light entering the room was controlled by the strip curtains on the window. Nora was not sure if there was even a proper name for that kind of curtains, but she only saw them at doctor's offices and similar places. There was a white desk by the window, with neatly arranged supplies that were within reach. Two chairs were lined up against the wall, on which many children were probably being scolded. In the corner was a beautiful purple flower that softened the formality of the whole room. The coat of arms of the Republic of Croatia stood on the wall, as in all the premises of state institutions, and behind the table sat a man who looked like he did not have long left until retirement. Only when he stood up to shake Nora's hand did she see how tall he was.

Gray-haired and in a shirt, bow tie, and business pants, he seemed stern and strong. He motioned Nora to sit down and returned to his chair. He did not smile much, but he had kind eyes. He looked like an aristocratic grandfather from the old American movies, who spends his free time with a Cuban cigar, a glass of whiskey, and a book.

- How are you?

- Great, thanks for asking – Nora replied with a smile.

- I am delighted you have decided to take this position, you will work with some great kids.

- Thank you for choosing me, I'm really excited to meet the little ones.

- Honestly, the reason we decided to take you was the topic of your thesis. Do you have any experience working with children who have behavioral disorders?

- I do not have any experience yet, but this is a topic that I have studied a lot and that I would like to continue pursuing.

- Great, we have a few students who have trouble concentrating, but they are not severe cases. These are children from the first to the fourth grade, so we would definitely like to find the learning methods that are best for them as soon as possible.

- I'm happy to have the opportunity to work with them. I'm sure those methods will have a significant impact on them.

- That's right. Thank you, Nora. The school secretary will contact you with all the information you need. I have to run to a meeting, see you on Monday.

Nora thanked him once again and walked out. She was so happy she could not stop smiling, and could not wait to tell Monika and Jana everything. On her way home, Nora stopped at a store to buy ice cream for the three of them to celebrate. She planned to spend the rest of the day searching for a preschool for Jana, and then she realized she had to talk to Vesna about the money. That thought immediately wiped the smile off her face, but Nora was convinced that all this was happening for some reason. Now, she was one step closer to living the life she wanted for herself and her daughter. Monika and Jana were waiting for her in the apartment all excited. Seeing them like that, Nora realized how important it was to share your happiness and pride with others. Those are the moments when everything gains more importance, and you get the strength that you need to continue down that path. When Jana fell asleep that evening, Nora sat down at her computer and began researching anything that might be useful to her in her new job. There was no way she would miss out on this opportunity.

19

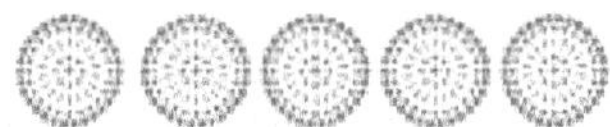

Nora was walking up the stairs to the fourth floor of the school. Her heart was beating fast as she was happily catching up with an older short woman, whose old gray tweed skirt was swaying with every step she took. She had foxy orange hair with small curls as remnants of a perm. She was not some kind or approachable woman, Nora would not even say she was particularly nice, but today she was Nora's favorite person in the whole world. She was taking her to the classroom to meet the children - her first workplace, and that was enough to fill Nora's heart with happiness and pride. With each step she climbed, she was closer to her dream coming true, the one for which she had invested years' worth of work and effort.

For that occasion, Nora wore her favorite baggy purple dress and black ankle boots, which she paired with a black sequined scarf. She was feeling beautiful and important. In a blink of a second, the images started flashing before her eyes – all those afternoons and evenings she had spent in the library, digging through books as she was studying for exams. Days and weeks of not going home, but instead sitting in an apartment writing papers and essays. The sleepless nights of worrying and dreading upcoming exams. It all came down to this moment, she was finally entering the world of working people. This was the first step of finally being her own boss.

They stopped in front of the classroom door with large collage letters forming 3D[39] on it. Nora was smiling from ear to ear. She followed the guidance counselor into the classroom and immediately glanced all around the room. It was unbelievable to her that she was finally here and that she would stay alone with these curious little kids in just a few moments. For a split second, she panicked, and her heart pounded high in her throat, threatening to burst out if she said anything. The counselor was opening her mouth and waved her finger, and Nora knew she was saying something, but she did not hear a sound from all the excitement she was feeling. Her head was already filled with her own heartbeats and her own thoughts, which sounded more like enthusiastic screams of delight. The next thing she saw was the counselor staring at her with a questioning look, along with twenty-four other curious pairs of eyes. She took a deep breath and looked around at the collective she would be the chief of for the next few months.

- Good day. My name is Nora, and I will be your teacher this year. I hope we will learn a lot together, have great fun, and enjoy all that awaits us — she was convinced that she had just grown a few centimeters from pride.

The children quickly accepted her. That was the thing she loved the most. They were so honest and full of acceptance because the world and life had not yet spoiled them. On her first workday, the first day of the school year, Nora decided to win them over. All of those college preparations, those hours spent in schools attending other teachers' classes, as well as the hours she held herself as a part of her curriculum, none of it was even similar to her being alone with these kids now, holding her own classes, and being the only one in charge. Nora was truly happy because she was confident and sure of herself, and was sure she was at the right place, right where she

---

39   Translator's note: Class department

needed to be. She enthusiastically began the preparations so she could teach those little smart brains as best as she could.

Her days were suddenly so filled, she barely had time to sleep. It was tiring, but she was content. The days when she did not know what to do with herself were behind her. The same as those days when she was worried about finding a job, all of it seemed so distant and unimportant now. She was off to the races. She was getting up early to get Jana ready for preschool and to cook lunch, so they have it ready when they got back home. Then, on her way to work, Nora would drop Jana off at preschool, kissing and hugging her. Saying goodbye was getting easier each day, and that gave Nora extra push and motivation to go on. She would be the first one to arrive at school, and she used that time to print everything she had prepared for her students the night before. Then, she would make herself a cup of coffee, sit down in the empty teachers' room and arrange her thoughts while waiting for the old and creaky printer to print out all twenty-four handouts in several copies.

Her apartment was filled with books that she used to get ideas for working with her students. She came up with worksheets, games, and educational stories that were supposed to help any student master the subject matter. It was exhausting work, but it was all worth it when she saw kids' enthusiasm about it, and how much it motivated them to study. It was not difficult for her to stay up late into the night after she had put Jana in bed so that she could get everything ready. It was not difficult to buy and carry a bunch of papers so that she could print out all the worksheets for her students. She felt lucky that the school, even though they did not have the blank papers, had at least a computer and a printer. She was gladly buying collage and glue every week, so they had something to do during the art class. She did not mind dragging her massive synthesizer from her college days along so they could have something to do during the music class. No, none of it was hard for her because she loved her work and knew that those children were worth it. In the end, it would all pay off. The children adored her, their parents were pleased with her,

her colleagues and the principal had only words of praise for her. She would certainly get a position full-time, she had to – everyone had noticed the effort she was putting into her work. That was the part she had control over, and she was determined to do it to the best of her ability.

She sipped the last sip of coffee. After working here for almost two months, her probationary period was about to come to an end. She would soon sign a contract, and everything would finally fall into place. The bell rang, and Nora quickly picked up all the papers, her laptop, and the projector, and hurried to the fourth floor.

*

- Are you saying that this position will be offered as vocational training? – Nora was skeptically looking at the principal. Her heart sank. She was hoping for a full-time job.

- Yes, yes. We have sent a request, and it was approved. We will issue the vacancy notice, and you will apply and surely be hired. Consider it done. Nothing will change – the principal looked at her over his thick glasses. Nora stared blankly at his mustache. Was she imagining it, or was the left side of his mustache longer than the right?

- Nothing will change except my salary. The vocational training wage is 2,400 kuna.

Nora started making calculations in her head – how would she support Jana and herself with such a salary?

- Yes, yes – the principal added quickly, peering somewhere above her head, acting as if he was in trouble.

- I know there is a difference compared with your current salary, but you know, it's more profitable for the school. The government pays for it, and we just have to accept what is better for the country. Nora nodded, still not knowing what to say. She was tugging the threads on her yellow scarf.

- It'll be over before you know it. Every start is difficult, my colleague. What's important is that you use the opportunity to work and gain experience – he said in an attempt to comfort her. Nora nodded again. She found herself nodding as she walked down the hallway from his office. This was a shock, Nora would have to find a way to fit all of hers and Jana's needs, their bills, preschool expenses into that new budget… It would be difficult, but she had it worse. Nora decided not to worry about it because she could not change anything, anyway. He was right about one thing, she needed to be working and gaining experience.

Nora stood by the blackboard and quietly looked around the classroom. They were writing a test, and all of their small hands were busy scribbling. She paced around the classroom and, with undisguised pride, watched them fill in almost all the blank boxes on their sheets. She was delighted to see that Ivan, who was not very interested in math so far, was adding up without much difficulty. That Renata, generally extremely talented in drawing, was leaving no lines blank in this math test. That Jasmina, who had math in her little finger, was solving extra credit tasks within the given time. Nora was watching them, each of them perceiving as her own. She was proud and pleased with her work. She managed to get everyone interested even in the subjects they had the worst results in. That just reinforced her theory that every child *can do and will do* if you encourage them in the right way. The noisy bell signaled the end of the class, as did the counselor's knock on the door. The principal was looking for Nora. She capered to his office, not at all concerned with what was about to happen. The application period for the vocational training position finished, and she knew she was the one who would be hired. After all, everyone told her so already, now they must have called her to sign a new contract. Nora hurriedly knocked on his door, hoping they could be done during the recess because she had biology class for which she had prepared little frogs and tadpoles. She spent the entire previous afternoon searching for them in the forest near the pool, where she took Jana for a walk.

- Come in, come in. Sit down.

A sudden change in the principal's approach had Nora raising her eyebrows. Why was he so flustered? Nora just sat in silence while the principal rummaged through some papers. He finally looked up when she began to impatiently squirm in the old tattered chair as if he had forgotten she was there.

- Yes, yes. Well, dear colleague, unfortunately, I have to tell you that another candidate was accepted for a vocational training position, that is, for the position you currently hold.

Nora opened her mouth and just stared at him. What was he saying? He continued to give her a pitying look before switching into a full pity mode and approaching her to pat her on the shoulder.

- Yes, yes. That means that you are no longer an employee of our school. These are the rules, the young man was a better candidate, and that must be respected. Yes, yes.

Nora was still just staring at him, unable to say anything. What was she supposed to say? Was she unemployed again? How? Why?

- A better candidate? – she finally managed to mutter so she would not seem completely mad.

- Yes, yes.

Nora got the urge to slap him across that big nose to make him stop saying that idiotic "yes, yes" in that idiotic tone as if she was a little girl who did not understand anything.

- You know, colleague, his mother has worked at our school for twenty-six years and is a great employee. Taking that into account, we are sure he will be too. Additionally, he is an active member of our community and participates in all kinds of events, both social and political.

Nora, still shocked, quickly closed her mouth. So that was the case. She was beaten by a party member. Unable to say anything, she just shook her head in disbelief, trying her best to stop the tears from welling up in her eyes. All her hard work was for nothing? All her will and passion were ultimately penalized? Did her results not matter? Did the kids' and parents' gratification not matter? Was her competence, or knowledge not important? It was hard to believe that the statement her parents often recited was still relevant: *those who were members of the Party*[40] *were always* better off. Nora refused to believe that. She found it impossible that something like this was happening to her in this day and age. And for the principal to admit that without any shame or qualms. That just cannot be normal.

- I'm not worried about you, my colleague. Such a good and skilled worker as you will surely find a new job quickly. Just not here with us, unfortunately. Yes, yes... - he cautiously showed Nora the way out. Their meeting was over. The door behind her was shut. She was unemployed again, and the reasoning was just the icing on this cake of absurdity.

She dragged herself home as if someone had beaten her. After crestfallenly packing up her things and feeling ashamed, she basically ran away so she would not have to say goodbye to her coworkers. She refused to accept that hard work meant nothing. That after such enthusiasm, happiness, and thrill of getting the first job, she was so harshly grounded. Since Nora left immediately after that unfortunate meeting, she had several hours to spare before picking up Jana from preschool. She used them to figure out how they would get by now that she did not even have even those 2,400 kuna. It was safe to say that Viktor would pay for preschool because Vesna was regularly sending Nora his money. Nora was planning to take that upon herself as well soon, but now she no longer had the opportunity to do so. She would still have to rely upon their "charity." Not once did Vesna ask if they needed any food or clothes, and Nora was too proud to mention that as long as they were scraping by with what little savings she had. It seemed like that would continue to be their reality — trying to

---

40   Communist Party of Yugoslavia

make ends meet and living off shopping center discounts. Soon, the overwhelming feeling of despair she had forgotten all about began to creep in again.

She was out of a job and had to again look for another one. Again, she would go on a crazy Internet search for vacancy listings, which would be impossible to find because it was November, and all of the vacancies were issued in September at the beginning of the school year. Again, she would have to visit the Employment Service and listen to their useless advice and suggestions. Again, she would have the group and individual interviews with her advisor. She would get extremely hopeful and then extremely disappointed over and over again. She was sad and did not want to go through that again. Again, she would dread the end of the month and opening the unpaid bill warnings and fearing how she would feed the two of them. Again, all those things that would be difficult for anyone to go through, and she would have to go through it on her own again.

At that moment, Nora could not help but feel resentment towards Viktor. She did not deserve this, and neither did her daughter. All these problems would be smaller and more manageable if there were two of them, fighting together. She would never forgive Viktor for leaving them so alone. Sadness quickly turned into anger, which was a good thing. In her case, it was a trigger to fight. She could not afford to give up. She would not surrender, she had Jana to think about. Her daughter would grow up as she had – happy and not lacking anything. Nora was sure they would rise above this.

What Nora did not quite expect was that it would happen so soon. A week later, the mom of one of her students called her and asked her to give him private lessons so that he would not fall behind.

- Robert was thrilled with you! He enjoyed studying because he knew his teacher Nora would be pleased and would commend him. Believe me, he has never been so happy and motivated to learn. Both his father and I were pleasantly surprised. When we heard the news about you leaving, we were shocked, all the parents were very appreciative of you – Zdenka told Nora over the phone, giving her ego a little boost.

- Thank you. I'm very glad to hear that, and it means a lot to me.

- That's the truth, my dear. Can you find the time to work with him a few afternoons a week? The price doesn't matter.

Nora thought about it for a moment. Why not? She could search the Internet to find out if she could register and start her own business. If she could not find a job, she could create one herself.

- Okay, I'll talk to you next week to figure out the details – Nora chirped happily into her phone. That afternoon, she and Jana put on the rubber boots and jumped on every puddle they came across. Jana was screaming with happiness, making Nora feel all mushy. Nothing could go wrong as long as they have each other.

It was 2 AM, and Nora was still surfing the Internet looking for some regulation that would benefit her and make her undertaking easier. Her third cup of coffee was almost empty. This country was simply preventing young people from succeeding. All the taxes, thousand different rules, and the saddest thing was that Nora had to read everything three times just so she could understand it. She has never felt more stupid. She threw away the fourth piece of paper, after crossing out another identical calculation. No matter how she tried to look at it, she could not start a business and live off, for now, one lesson. She tried to calculate how many lessons she should be giving to make it worthwhile, and the number seemed extremely large. Plus, she was not sure if there even were so many elementary-school children whose parents would be willing to pay for private lessons. Yes, that would be a good side income, but as a primary source of livelihood, not so much. She refreshed the Service website as if there would be new vacancies published at 2 in the morning. Glancing over it, she saw as many as six listings for vocational training, but she had already applied for each of them. Nothing else was offered. All schools really went crazy about vocational training.

It was a miserable opportunity, and even for that, you obviously needed a connection. She frowned sadly at the screen. The screen light was the only light in the darkened room, and Jana's quiet and rhythmic breathing had such a soporific effect that it took Nora only a few moments to fall asleep over her computer, with her head smashed against the keyboard. She dreamed that everything was fine. She dreamed she was happy.

20

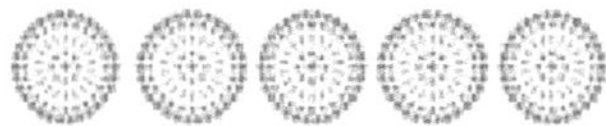

- Thank you for coming, we will definitely contact you as soon as we're done with all the interviews.

- Thank you for the opportunity. Have a beautiful day – Nora said with a completely fake smile on her face. But she had to fake it for the interviews. Who in their right mind would hire a person who does not care about leaving a good impression? Who would employ a desperate person?

She came out of another interview and felt miserable. She would spend the rest of that day mechanically doing chores around the house. Feeling terrible, Nora did not want to talk to anyone or do anything, she just wanted to sleep. She could feel that she was holding back the tears, and that made her scared depression would crush her again. She must not allow herself that, but could she even fight it? Jana was refusing to put on her pajamas because she knew that meant going to bed soon. As soon as Nora managed to slip her on the second pajama leg, Jana ran into the kitchen like a bullet. She wanted to play, but Nora just did not have any strength left. She could feel every heartbeat and the pressure in her lungs. Her head was hot, and she lacked air. She just wanted to run out into the cold and let it all out. Nora wished somebody shook her so she could forget everything and start all over. She was afraid of not able to do this alone and that her daughter would suffer if anything went wrong. All night long, Nora was in and out of some damn half-sleep, sweaty and panicking. Was she losing her mind? What to do next? She finally fell asleep an hour before Jana woke her up in the morning.

Today was one of the three days of the week she was going to see Robert. She helped him with studying and writing homework that he had problems doing on his own. His mom Zdenka would pick him up from school and wait for Nora with him in their apartment, after which she would return to work. They lived in a beautiful apartment on the west side of the city surrounded by greenery and trees. The interior was decorated with brown and white combinations, and the whole apartment looked like something out of a magazine. Their living room was equipped with the latest technological appliances. Nora did not know what half of them are for. In front of the balcony was a large table with eight chairs around it, always stylishly decorated. The thing Nora liked the most was the kitchen. There was a vast empty space in the middle of it, and the whole room was lit by natural light. There were so much space and so much cooking equipment that even if hot dogs were the only thing you knew how to prepare, you would want to cook in that kitchen. One of the walls was entirely painted blue with an image of a branch with water droplets on it. The motif itself was not anything special, but you could not walk through that kitchen and not look at it. Nothing in that apartment was out of place, but then, Nora walked into Robert's room.

There was a sea of toys on the floor, but Robert moved through them as if they were exactly where they were supposed to be. The first time she was here, Nora observed his behavior both while he was playing and while he was studying. He was a great kid, but he had a completely misguided view of studying, doing homework, and going to school. Robert perceived it as punishment, but in fact, he was an inquisitive child who enjoyed learning. Nora noticed that he would turn each toy in 10 different ways and that every time he was playing, he managed to come up with a new purpose for the same toy, so it could fit the game he had imagined. So Nora decided to design his tasks the same way. Together, they came up with a game where each task represented one level of a game. Between each assignment, he had special missions that required him thinking, and this helped him concentrate on learning. Nora enjoyed working with him. He would sit at his desk in his room, entirely focused on the sheet in front of him, and the moment he would come across the problematic part, he would start twirling his brown locks with a pencil. Robert had dark brown eyes and gorgeous thick long lashes. His eyes could not hide his interest in something, and he would smile mysteriously every time he knew he was doing something right. He was a cheerful kid that was assessed by the school as a high-energy child, unable to focus for prolonged periods.

- Hello! – Zdenka shouted cheerfully as she walked into the apartment with four bags in each hand. Robert finished all his assignments and was just showing Nora his new toy, but as soon as he heard his mom, he went to greet her. At first, Zdenka could seem like a strict businesswoman, but that initial coldness would disappear as soon as she heartily laughed. Zdenka had the same eyes as Robert and beautiful features. You could tell she took care of her appearance, and she looked gorgeous. She was well-groomed, and the straight, brown hair up to her shoulders, as well as the fashionable gray, black, and brown combinations, suited her perfectly.

- Hi, mom! – Robert ran towards her as Nora was packing up her things.

- Hi, honey, how was it?

- Great, I've crossed the last level fastest so far.

- Okay? – she said questioningly and looked at Nora.

- He was great, we went over everything.

- Good job, kiddo.

- Zdenka, could I ask you for a favor?

- Please, don't be so formal. Come on, ask.

- I have a job interview on Wednesday, so I was hoping if I could come an hour later?

- Sure, no problem. And good luck, I hope someone will recognize what you are capable of achieving in your work with kids. But that doesn't mean we're losing you, right?

- Thank you for that, it means a lot to me. And I would certainly like to keep coming here because I applied for a vocational training position.

Nora received a resolution of that interview that Wednesday, just as she was leaving their apartment. They chose her. Finally! She got a job for the whole year. For one full year, she would have at least some money she can count on. Plus the lessons. Immediately she was enthusiastic and felt that rush of happiness she had not felt in so long. This could be her chance. And as slim as it was, she was going to grab it. She would do anything she had to become irreplaceable in that job. She had a year to prove to them that they would be crazy to let her go. Yes, that was going to be her mindset from now on. She just had to make the best out of her financial situation for a year, and then everything would slowly fall into place.

Three full months have passed since they had selected her for a vocational training program as a supervisor at an all-day school, and Nora was still waiting for approval so she could start working. Three months! She was done; she was losing her patience and just waited for the day she would snap. After finishing a lesson with Robert, she had a little time before she needed to pick up Jana, so she decided to go to the Employment Service. She was willing to type that one damn paper she needed herself. *I mean, even if they were carving it in stone, it should have been done by now!*

She arrived at the building in front of which she had been a hundred times before. She had a strange habit of remembering totally unnecessary things when she was angry. So now, for example, she knew that there were 7 steps and 5 red pillars in front of the entrance, the walls were burgundy, and the white doors seemed to invite street artists to paint graffiti on them. The walls inside, where all the magic for the unemployed happened, were white, while clerk counters, doors, desk, and chairs were blue. They decided to put the red pillars inside as well, perhaps to make the interior look more cheerful. There was a bulletin board at the entrance that was so full you would think they are actually offering that many jobs. But for the most part, it was just a few ads with added laws, regulations, and articles. She walked in, saw the free counter, and immediately made her way toward an older woman with short brown hair, big glasses, and a face that looked like it had not smiled for a long time. When she saw Nora standing in front of her, she rolled her eyes and looked back at the paper she was filling at a snail's pace.

- Good afternoon — Nora said first and was met with silence. The lady continued filling in her paper with no indication she had heard Nora.

- Good day — Nora repeated.

- Just a second, miss. I'm in the middle of something if you haven't noticed.

- Don't mind me, I was just making sure you heard me — Nora replied in an equally polite tone.

- How can I help you? — the woman said, blowing air out after literally every word, probably to make sure Nora knew how displeased she was with the fact that Nora picked her counter. Now, she would get to see just how much Nora did not care about it.

- I have a question regarding vocational training approval. How long does it take to get this approval, that is, what is the legal deadline within which approval must be resolved?

- 50 business days – she sighed again. *God, how much excess air does this woman have?*

- I've been waiting for three months.

- We can't do anything until we receive approval from Zagreb.

- I don't care. You have to be able to do something, anything. You are paid to do something, right? Aren't you a branch office of the Employment Service? Yes, you are. Aren't you here to be the connection between the Service and me? Yes, you are. So please do something and find out when I can expect my approval.

- I can send an e-mail – the woman said so disinterestedly it was almost an insult. It was evident that she was not going to send anything to anyone, because why would she? That was not in her job description, so why should she care about someone's job?

- Fine, I know you won't. Congratulations, you won, lady. Can I get some written confirmation that you, an official, have told me that the maximum waiting time for approval is 50 business days?

- Why do you need confirmation? It's all stated in the Law – she was getting increasingly more frustrated with this conversation.

- Oh, okay. So if it's in the Law, that's the way it should be, right? How come then I am still waiting for it long after the deadline had passed if it's in the fucking Law? Is there anything I can do about it?

- You cannot. It will arrive when it arrives. I don't know what else to tell you – she said and continued filling in that damn paper Nora wanted to take and tear into a thousand pieces.

And that was that. End of conversation. Nora stormed out downright furious and out of her mind. How was this possible? How mad could you be at a person you did not even know; how angry could you be with a country, a program, a system? Pff, you could get as angry as you want, and it would not matter. Nothing would change. Nora wondered would it be easier for her if the woman at that counter was nicer. Not that it would make her situation any better or change the fact that this was happening, and no one could do anything about it, but at least she would feel like someone cared.

*

Nora spent another evening online. Without a clear idea of what she was searching for, she ended up on a forum where people shared their experiences with the vocational training program. She read their stories, comments, questions, and advice, all coming from young people who had gone through the same crap as she had. So many of them left everything behind and fled the country because they had been driven to the brink. It was saddening to read the headlines mentioning figures higher than 36,000 people who emigrated in 2016 alone, mostly young people aged between 20 and 39. All that information brought tears to Nora's eyes.

She could not believe all the different things people had to put up with just by living in this country. One guy on the forum commented about the abolition of transportation compensation if you were not traveling by public transport. He lived in a county where the public transport network was underdeveloped, so the earliest bus was at 2:30 PM and the one to get back at 10 PM. His working hours were from 8 AM to 4 PM, and the bus station was seven kilometers away. One girl wrote that she finished two majors; in other words, she had two professions. For each of them, she had to pass the state exam, which meant she had to go through the vocational training program. Since you could only go through this program once, she had to choose which profession she would give up. You could not count all the comments and experiences on that forum, there were so many of them. It was horrible.

And then Nora found footage of an HRT[41] show that featured a girl who was one of the organizers of the announced protest against this measure, and a deputy director of the Employment Service. Two

---

41   Croatian Radiotelevision

different sides of the same story and their respective arguments. Nora could not believe the things being said on national television, or that this woman was sitting there defending the program with arguments that were supposed to sound commendable. After hearing the statement that the Government was doing everything in its power to restore the young person's dignity, Nora was sure there was nothing else that could surprise her. When asked how many people had been employed after vocational training, this woman offered no answer. She continued by saying that 5,000 people were currently in the vocational training program, and 3,000 were in the active employment policy program. That was not even close to answering the question she had been asked, but, well, she said it. On national television. And after making that statement, she probably returned to her job. And there, they probably congratulated her and thank her for agreeing to go on television to defend the program.

Nora moved away from the screen and closed all the tabs. All the articles, Facebook comments, YouTube channels with interviews with the politicians, that forum, and everything else mentioning vocational training without employment. She opened a new Word document and began writing a letter. A letter that she would never send to anyone, not because of fear or shame, but because she knew it would not change anything. She was writing it for every politician who had ever stood in front of cameras and defended this program.

Dear Sir/Madam,

I am starting my letter this way out of common decency my mom has taught me because I actually don't have any respect for you. My name and age don't matter, neither do my life circumstances. It doesn't matter where I live or how I look, or anything else that could help you imagine me. If you wish, I could be a young person you will disregard from the start and label as a loudmouth brat. Or I could be an old woman who just really likes to patronize everyone. But you know who else I could be? Your daughter. But none of that matters because either way, I am a part of that bunch that you should care about.

How are you not ashamed? How come you don't find it difficult to stand in front of the cameras and say those things, knowing that I'm watching? How do you not feel bad addressing me that way? How can you defend, out loud, a program that brings me to the brink of destitution?

I know you know how much I had put into my education. I know you know how hard I worked. I know you know how good I can be at my job and how much I love doing it. I know you know how motivated and willing I am to make a change. I know you know all of that! So how can you then allow someone to hire me for a wage of 2,620 kuna, without any recognition for my work? How can you let them do that to me?

Do you think you would be able to slap me if I were standing in front of you? To slap me across the face, hurting me physically, but also mentally, as the slap was supposed to humiliate me. Do you think you could do that to me? You are doing exactly that every time you say something in front of the cameras or in an assembly hall or during lunch with your colleagues, or when making decisions or while creating programs and laws. How can you humiliate me like that? How can you humiliate anyone like that? What is wrong with you?

Take a look at your life. How long does it take you to spend 2,620 kuna? You mean to tell me that should be enough for me to have a roof over my head, to eat, sleep, and raise my child? How come you are not saddened by my tears? How come you don't care if I leave? How do you not understand that if I go like everyone else, there would no longer be anyone to support the lifestyle you got so used to by now? How is it even possible that you don't see that? You live in the most beautiful country in the world, with people who would unite as one in a split second if you needed help. Yes, even you, even after everything you've ruined. So many people would help you in your time of need that it would make your heart explode with all the love and happiness. I am all those people.

Do you even care about me?

21

After four months of waiting for approval, Nora finally began working as an associate teacher in one all-day elementary school. She was given her own little classroom, which was obviously improvised for the purposes of this new program. There were three small desks in that classroom, each for four children, and the walls were decorated with children's drawings. The walls were painted yellow, while three shelves held all the props the school provided – a ream of blank paper, several picture books, coloring books, crayons, markers, watercolors, and paintbrushes. All in all, not too much, but with a little imagination, it could all be turned into something cool. The school worked in two shifts, so that meant that Nora's morning group of students, who were first and second-graders, had classes in the afternoon, and her afternoon shift consisted of third and fourth-graders who had their classes in the morning.

In those two small groups, Nora could already see big little people. There was a boy who worshiped the numbers. Whenever he learned a new math thing, he could not stop talking about it. Nora was fascinated by how he was able to assign a number to any object he saw. There was also a girl who kept taking coloring books, and instead of coloring, she would come up with her own stories. Another girl, who felt really strongly about colors, tried to explain to the first girl that she did not know how to properly play with coloring books. Nora could not wait for a moment in her life when she would be able to read that little girl's book, with the front cover designed by the one who loves coloring, of course. One boy would draw a spider on every blank piece of paper he would come across. Another boy, a second-grader, was consistently acting tough. He did not want to do anything, and according to him, everything was stupid. Until Nora turned on the music. He was immediately faced with a dilemma whether to give in to his desire to dance, or to stay cool, leaning against the corner wall as his older brother taught him.

Nora loved her new job. She was so committed to working hard with these kids that everyone, from other teachers to parents and children, started believing in her work methods. She really did care about them, and even that little bit of attention she devoted to them, unburdened by the school curriculum, allowed her to help them learn better.

After work, Nora would return home to her beautiful baby, who was growing up right before her eyes. Jana was starting to look more like Viktor every day. Whenever Nora thought about him, she got sad; she would remember how good he was, how much he loved her at one point in their lives. Nora would also remember how much she loved him. She would remember the way he took care of her, the way he protected her, how gentle and funny, and understanding he was. But then, she would also remember how long it had been since Jana saw him. And then, she would get angry. Everyone should be ready for anything from anyone in their lives, but Nora was certainly not ready for that. She never expected that from Viktor. They were in contact only out of courtesy, he would reach out and ask about Jana, and Nora would send him a photo. She knew that he was regularly talking to Vesna and that he was informed about everything that was going on, but she did not know how to feel about that. Nora was not sure for how long she would be able to keep that up, hoping that he would come to his senses and come back home. Not because of her, that was over; Nora was sure she would never be able to trust him or rely on him again, and that she would always remember the pain he caused her. He was far from the person she had fallen in love with, but Nora was aware that none of that mattered or was necessary for him to be a good father that Jana deserved. Jana was the sole reason Nora wanted Viktor to come back home, and for them to have a good relationship.

It had been six months since she started working, and she has been feeling more comfortable and confident in her work every day. First of all, she was proud of herself. Her kids' achievements and all the praise from her coworkers and parents kept her motivated. What did not motivate her was her salary. It was ridiculous and humiliating in every regard, but Nora decided not to look at it that way at all. She had what she had, plus some extra from giving extra lessons to Robert. Viktor was sending her money for Jana's preschool, fortunately, because Nora would not be able to cover that amount herself in any way, nor the apartment they were living in. But she knew that was not going to last forever, so she had a clear vision and was sure there was a way to make something happen out of it.

- Are you worried about something, you look worried? – one of her colleagues asked her when it was just the two of them in the teacher's room.

- No, I just don't understand the salary figure from last month. The amount has been reduced by about 116 kuna, and I'm not sure why – Nora said with a raised eyebrow.

- Did you take any of your vacation days?

- Yeah, sure, I went on a trip around the world with this salary of mine – Nora replied sarcastically and laughed.

- I wasn't here one Friday when Jana got sick, but that can't be it.

- Unfortunately, my dear, it can. My brother is on vocational training; they deduct one daily wage from your pay for every sick day you take.

- I actually knew about that, for the matter of fact, but I guess it didn't occur to me. Yeah, it makes sense, it's the amount of a daily wage and 7 kuna for transportation.

Nora could not believe it. Actually, she could not believe she did not believe it. Why was she still surprised by all of this?

- For real, if it wasn't so sad, it would be funny. But don't worry, you're soon done with this stupid vocational thing, and everything will be different.

- Right, I'll be unemployed again. I love change.

- No way! There is not one person who is not happy with your work. I can't imagine the wonders you would do if you had the whole class department for yourself.

- Thank you, but not so fast. Until that happens, though, I'll still be on a lookout for another job.

- I understand, yes, but I really believe they will keep you. Oh, I forgot to ask you, did Davor's mom call you?

- Snježana? I saw a missed call and completely forgot about it, it was probably her. I'm going to go call her to see what it was about.

Davor was a boy with severe ADHD, but this was not talked about, and Nora was certainly not the person that should make that diagnosis. Besides disrupting the class, he could not concentrate on assignments, he was loud and would interrupt every time somebody else would talk. He had been considered a misbehaved child since preschool, he was always told to calm down or was grounded. There was no worse torture for him than standing in a corner during some game or activity that he did not participate in. He would stand there screaming and crying, so while he was grounded, nobody could really get anything done. Nora knew precisely what the possible consequences of such methods could be, and she was sad that Davor was not one of the children coming to her all-day program. His mom, Snježana, heard about Nora from another mom and wanted to see if Nora could possibly work with Davor out of class. Nora agreed because that was exactly what she wanted to do in her life, and some extra money certainly would not hurt. Her week was now completely booked, but Nora was happy to have the privilege of doing what she loved. At home, she further looked into ADHD as a behavioral disorder and recognized a lot of symptoms Davor had, at least according to her colleagues. He had to keep moving, but if he was supposed to sit still, he had to at least do something with his hands. He had impulsive and unpredictable reactions, and would often get into trouble. He was moody, and all of that was a part of a reason why he did not have a lot of friends. He was lonely and was consistently blamed for something, which had a terrible effect on his confidence, even at such an early age.

The principal called Nora to his office a month before her contract was supposed to end because he wanted to tell her on time that they would not be able to keep her. The Ministry of Science and Education has granted them vocational training for the next year, and that kind of employment was much more cost-effective for them. He was sorry because he recognized how committed she was to her work and how pleased the parents were with her. The saddest thing was that she could tell he was genuine, but he had to leave it at that.

Nora anticipated a full-blown panic or chocking attack, or at least feeling pressure in her lungs. She assumed she would cry or scream, or have any kind of reaction, but she was just silent. She thanked him and walked out of his office, took her things, and left school. Disappointed and with a crushed spirit. Fully aware that she was no longer even a vocational training candidate, she could assume how the next lookout for a job would look like. How was it even possible for her to stand and walk right now, she wondered, walking around the city she genuinely grew to love. Her head was completely empty, and she felt like a madman experiencing a nervous breakdown.

She was on her way to her lesson with Davor, but she was worried about being able to do anything with him, considering her current state. She found him in his room nervously finishing some toy. His short brown hair was framing his little symmetrical face. He would always observe and examine something intensely, and Nora had a feeling that at the age of 12, this kid would probably have those little wrinkles between the eyebrows that you get when you are angry or contemplate about something all the time. He had straight teeth and a charming smile, which, unfortunately, Nora did not get to see very often. He made a toy for her so that immediately improved her mood and made her smile. *Okay, Nora, you know that it's not your fault that they fired you. You have done everything humanly possible and given your all. That's what counts.*

That night Nora was watching the TV while Jana was playing with a toy Davor had made. Only then did Nora realize what he had actually made. At first, the toy looked like a bunch of ice cream sticks tied together with some colorful string, but as Jana tugged at those sticks, they began to form a path meant for a small metal ball that Davor had placed in the middle. Nora took the toy from Jana and started examing it. She could not believe it! The amount of concentration it would take for anyone to make something like this, especially for a child with ADHD. Nora could only imagine how happy and pleased with himself Davor was. That was exactly what she needed! A sign that she had to do this for the rest of her life, no matter the cost!

After thinking back at everything they had been doing together, Nora started to list out loud all the methods that possibly helped Davor and made him capable of designing something like this. She tried to single out a specific task or a game they had played, but she quickly realized that it was all connected. Everything started falling into place. All the children she had the opportunity to meet were going through her mind, especially those demonstrating some changes in their behavior. Nora could visualize an exact approach she would use on each of them to help them reach their full potential. She was going to create a place to help children like Davor, and this place was going to be called Leap of faith.

She began to lay down a plan and write down all the questions she could think of. She decided that it would be best to work with eight children at first, in two groups of four. She was going to find out what kept them focused and was going to use that to present them with any subject matter they had to deal with. Her program would not be related to, or be defined by, the school curriculum, but her work would directly affect and improve children's abilities to keep up with the school program. That is, since she was convinced that these kids were actually geniuses, she hoped that the school program would be able to keep up with them.

She was elated and excited. This was it! Nora has never felt this feeling before. At the moment in her life when everything seemed to be falling apart, when she had nothing to look forward to, and by all indications, was not far away from a mental breakdown, Nora believed she finally found a solution. Not only did she believe it, but she was also convinced it would work. She was jumping all around the apartment like a crazy person before noticing that Jana fell asleep in the armchair.

- Oh, come on, Nora! You fool! How are you so lucky to have such a good kid?

She carried Jana to her bed and sat by her side for a few minutes. The greatest blessing of her life. Overwhelmed with a real sense of happiness, peace, and gratitude, Nora smiled. It was a smile that is much harder to wipe off than any tear, so at that moment, she was grateful that was the way it was. Nora believed, with every cell in her body, that she would finally be able to fulfill the promise she had made to her daughter. She thought to check the laws governing such an institution, but she stopped herself on her way to the computer.

- Nora, you are smart enough to know that checking and researching the Law will only make you annoyed – she said to herself, then lay down next to Jana, and fell asleep never happier.

The next day, she was supposed to go to Davor's again, so she brought the toy he made to thank him. He was ecstatic that she figured how the toy worked. Among everything, Nora was equally astonished by the fact he had let her figure it out on her own. After their lesson, Snježana invited her to stay for coffee, which Nora gladly accepted. Snježana was a young mom, and it was apparent how tired she was. She usually wore jeans and a T-shirt over which she would put on a sweatshirt or a plaid shirt. Although she was not all dressed-up, she radiated a natural beauty. Snježana had a lot on her plate with work and Davor, so being tired slowly became a part of her daily look. Her husband was as busy as she was, and Nora had only seen him several times, and only for a few minutes.

Nora was not even sure how it all began, but suddenly she was telling Snježana all about her idea. She seemed so excited and motivated that Snježana could only admire her, considering she witnessed firsthand what Nora was capable of. She wanted to let Nora know that what she had achieved with her son in just a few months, no one had ever come even close. Snježana had no doubt that Nora was put on this Earth to do exactly that. And that was what she told her when Nora stopped to catch her breath as she was presenting her idea so vigorously, like a kid telling their mom the best thing that has ever happened to them. When she heard what Snježana had to say, Nora started crying.

She was embarrassed to be whining in the woman's kitchen, but she could not help it. She did not even realize how much she needed someone to understand her and to be by her side no matter what. Snježana mentioned her friend Ana, who started her own business and should have some helpful tips for Nora, even though she had opened a foreign language school. Nora did not have a clue where to even begin, but she was confident it would work out. And when you believe in something, the universe usually takes care of everything else.

22

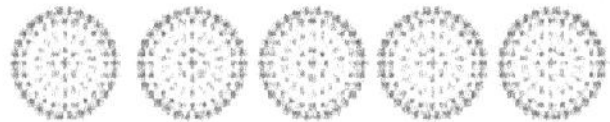

Her head was throbbing from all the contradictory information she was receiving. Nora has been struggling for days, reading all the regulations and experiences of other people, and could not say that she was any smarter than she was before. Quite simply, none of it made any sense, no rhyme or reason to any of the information she had found. She kept running around in circles, and that made her progressively more frustrated. Nora was getting more irritable and did not have the patience for anything. When she went crazy over Jana spilling crayons out of a plastic bucket, a frightened look on her daughter's face made her take a step back. *What is the matter with me? What have I turned into? Is this what our life is going to be like? Me raving at my child because she's a child? Neither she nor I was to blame for this situation, nor can we do anything about it.*

The tears ran down Nora's cheeks as she was picking up the crayons from the floor. In an attempt to make a better life for them, she was creating a toxic atmosphere all around them. She was no longer devoted to Jana, she was absent-minded, nervous, frustrated because none of the officials behind those counters had any information, because all of this was taking so long. She was sad because her own country was preventing her from turning her idea into reality. She was tired of everything. When Nora picked up the last crayon, Jana had already forgotten about Nora's outburst and was watching a cartoon on the TV. Nora went to some drawer and dug through it until she pulled out a small envelope with green flowers on it. It was a gift certificate for a massage that Monika had gifted her for her birthday, and that has since been collecting dust at the bottom of a kitchen drawer that Nora used for all kinds of different random things. *That's exactly what I need to pull myself together*, she thought.

- Stop getting on my nerves! It's not my first time babysitting her. If anything happens, I'll call you. Now go, it's about time you relaxed a bit. You are making all of us nervous.

Monika literally pushed Nora out the door and slammed it in her face.

Nora took a long way to the parlor, enjoying the fresh air and breathing slowly and deeply. She felt as if she was turning into an old spinster frustrated with her life. She was not going to allow the system to defeat her again, to steal her dignity and the right to the life she had imagined for herself and Jana. If she had learned anything by now, it was how not to give up.

The massage parlor was beautifully peaceful. All the lights were dimmed, there were tealights on the dressers, and the smell in the air was sweet and relaxing. A friendly girl, younger than Nora, led her into a completely dark room, and in it, a tune that mimicked the sound of the sea, birds, and crickets was playing in the background. Nora lay down on a table in the middle of the room and decided she would try to completely clear her head. This was her time. One whole hour just for her. She could hear the girl pouring some oil on her hands before she started gently massaging Nora's back in circular motions, putting pressure at all the right spots. Nora felt like she was on cloud nine.

An hour later, she hurried home. How could she be so silly and forget about Snježana giving her Ana's number? She remembered it about halfway through the massage, probably because her mind was so clear and free to wander around. She had to call her as soon as possible and arrange a meeting. Nora obviously did not know what the hell she was doing; she needed someone experienced, someone who could specifically tell her where to start, and what to pay attention to. All the wasted days and weeks trying to figure it out on her own, and all the while, she had someone to reach out to, someone who had gone through a similar situation. *I will never again dare to think that massages, or any self-care services, are a waste of money,* she thought with a smile, much more relaxed and fulfilled.

Nora sat back in a red think armchair in a vintage coffee shop. She arrived early because she was too excited to wait at home. She ordered a large cup of hot chocolate because nothing could go wrong if you had a double dose of that liquid gold within reach. The table Nora was sitting at was antique with tiny engravings. Nora traced the shape of a rose with thorns with her finger.

- Hi! It's nice to finally meet you in person. I am Ana.

A short, red-headed woman with a big smile offered Nora her hand. Her eyes were brown and lively, and they made her seem playful as they shifted from object to object at an astonishing speed. She sat down next to Nora and grabbed her hands without any restraint.

- Your dress is gorgeous, it brings out your complexion and your eyes so well.

Nora was, for a moment, taken aback by Ana's directness and frankness. This was the first time they saw each other in person, and until now, they had only spoken over the phone. Looking at her sincere smile, Nora smiled too. This beautiful woman was selflessly offering her help. It seemed as though the sky still had a couple of spare good things to send your way in the time of need.

- It's good to finally see you. You don't know how much this means to me – Nora reciprocated Ana's contagious enthusiasm.

- Then let's not keep you waiting any longer. I'm listening, what do you want to know? And don't hesitate to be more particular than over the phone – Ana said and waved to the waiter, motioning she would have the same as Nora.

- Hot chocolate is best for brain work – she winked at Nora and leaned back in an armchair that was so huge in comparison to her that she completely sank into it.

- I don't even know where to start. I have an idea, I have a will to make it happen, but that is as far as I've come. I would like to open a daycare center for children who have certain behavioral disorders. I want to tailor a particular method of learning for each of them. The thing that concerns me – everything else. I don't know where to start, how to open a business? Should it be a private business at all? Or a liberal profession? What papers do I need? What charges should I pay? I mean, I don't wanna be locked down for some tax evasion or something. Who can I contact, actually, who should I contact, what institutions do I have to inform? And similar. If you understood anything at all.

- Of course, I did. I went through the same thing. After receiving completely different information from several different officials doing the exact same job, I gave up on looking for information that way. Instead, I went to… And you will laugh, but desperate times call for desperate measures. So, I went to a political rally.

- A political rally? – Nora was skeptical about that information.

- Okay, I really didn't expect that.

- Yeah, I know it sounds weird, but it was pre-election time, and everyone's mouths were full of hiring young people, helping young people, encouraging young people, and similar slogans. So I thought, *okay, Ana, what do you have to lose?* I got there and asked a question. I don't even know where did I get the courage, my guess is desperation. I raised my hand and asked the most prominent candidate a question, the one about whom all the newspapers were buzzing and who was ahead in all the polls. I asked him what his concrete plans about the young people not being able to get a job or start their own business were. He answered me the way all politicians do; he talked in circles, beating around the bush. I was ready to engage in an endless discussion with him and risk getting thrown out of the rally, which would be rock bottom even for a desperate person. But then Ema approached me, a young woman who worked on his campaign, and offered me help. Specifically, she told me about the incentives to which I was entitled and instructed me on which door to knock to make it happen. I learned that, first of all, you need to talk to an accountant. That is the best way for you to understand all the pros and cons of all types of businesses. Your first step should be to find out exactly what you already said, and that is whether you should open a business, a d.o.o.[42], a j.d.o.o.[43], or some similar letters. When you decide on that, you should go collect all the papers. That is a never-ending process, and you should be fully prepared for that. You will always, but always, miss some other piece of paper. I would further advise you to speak with an expert who is involved in the absorption of EU Funds. I'll give you a number of a guy I worked with. He's great, he works on the principle that you pay only if you get the funds, and if you don't, you only have to pay for the costs of collecting all those papers.

Ana talked nonstop for an hour, while Nora wrote everything down. She had received so much useful information that she was in awe how Ana spoke about it and handled it so effortlessly. The thing that mattered the most to Nora was that now she had Ana, that is, someone who was ready to help at any time if she got stuck.

Now, there was a solid plan of action to get her idea going. She figured out how her game plan would look like. And at that moment, while she was drinking hot chocolate with one of the best types of people, the one who would selflessly share their knowledge, that was

---

42   Limited liability company

43   Simple limited liability company

when Nora decided to open her own business and that there was no going back from it.

*

Nora took a sip of the beer she was forced to order. They had been sitting here for an hour, and she only drank one-third of the bottle, doubting it would get any better. The only thing she could say for sure was that she worked up an appetite, which was confirmed by the loud noises coming from her stomach.

- I would've much more preferred that tea – Nora gave Dajana an accusing look, while she was just staring at her in astonishment.

- Aaaaaaaand? Did you forget what happened next or…?

- Nothing happened next – another forced sip, accompanied by the funny expression on her face.

- That was actually just a few days ago, and the thing I'm going to do next is - start my new adventure. According to my own rules.

- Nora, you pleasantly surprised me! You're no longer the Nora we knew in high school! You're neither whiny nor weepy, nor dependent, nor timid! Really, well done, you've made a real 180 – Veronika seemed genuinely moved.

- Bloody hell, enough with this sentimental crap, all we need is for you to get all mushy now. We could eat something, huh? My sister told me that some new place called Crafter opened recently and that they often munch there – Sofija was pulling out her phone to order. When it came to her sister's opinion, there was never a shred of doubt in her mind that it could be anything but perfect.

- Before you go and ravage the entire menu, let me just tell you that I am that Ema and that I remember that lady like it was yesterday… That was my first day of work!

Four dumbfounded heads turned in her direction, while Ema wistfully stared at their old school through the window. The mere sight of that grand building brought back so many memories. Each window reminded her of the subject they had in that specific classroom. Ground floor, three windows in a row on the right side of the building, an English class when Goran threw his phone out the window so the professor could not find it. A view of the middle floor, a classroom in the middle, a chemistry class, and them fooling around in the professor's rolling chair. And finally, a view of the classroom on the top floor where, right after this adventure with chairs, they spent two periods listening to their homeroom professor's tirade on their bad behavior and how she was going to knock those shenanigans right out of their heads.

- No way!

- You're shitting me! – Sofija was the loudest.

- Obviously, not everything has changed. You, Sofija, are still a sailor – Veronika grinned, but Sofija just shrugged her off, eager to hear what Ema had to say.

- Why are you not speaking already? Talk, woman!

Ema looked away from the school and turned to girls who looked like a bunch of kids who had just been promised a full bag of candy. Their eyes wide open, but their mouths even wider, so much that it seemed they were going to start drooling any second. She knew instantly that nothing had changed in these ten years, and that they were still the same girls who had each other, who were there for each other and, most importantly, who understood each other. Only now they were women, genuine, kind, and warm women. Her girlfriends. Well, okay! If anyone should hear her story, then it should be them. This is where she wants to keep her integrity.

- It might not be such a bad idea to eat something first. It's a long story…

Something about us
and to whom we are thankful

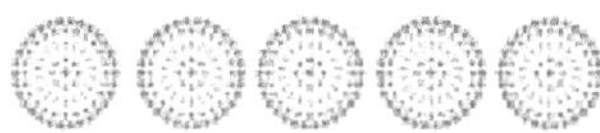

Considering there is two of us, we are going to split this part up a bit because there is a lot we would like to say. And because it wouldn't make any sense for this part to be one half of the entire book, we had to take it down a notch.

So, first up is Marina, with something to say about Nataša. Nataša is a girl I went to high school with, and although we are different in every possible way, the one thing we agree on is definitely books. She is a chemical engineer and adores that chemistry, which I never entirely understood, but okay. She is married and has a wonderful little son, my godchild, who will have to know this book by heart, from cover to cover. Of all the people I'm about to thank, I start with her because if it wasn't for her, something I've been dreaming about for my entire life would have never happened. She has a unique way of calming me down, lots of different ways to make me laugh, and she is my book soulmate.

Other special people who have been by my side this entire time are my parents, who I love more than anyone else in this world, and who are not even aware of how much they have given me.

No one in the world loves me more than my dad, he would come running in a second if I asked. And my mom would tag along with him. She is the first person to read everything I write, and she would search the world for anything I could possibly need. I am thankful to my brothers and the rest of my family, who are very proud of me, which I find very pleasant. I have amazing people around me who have shared every part of this book with me, and I will be eternally grateful to them, with all my heart. And what's even more important, I know they are aware of that. Thank you, Marina, Iva, Iva, Matea, Lucija, and Lidija ("k89mshl") for being understanding about absolutely everything since day one – if it weren't for you, I'm not sure what would have happened to my head. Thank you, "little girls," thank you to all of you with whom I worked and to all of you who came into my life for whatever reason. I know you all belong here.

Now it is Nataša's turn, with something to say about Marina, for starters. Marina is the type of person anyone would want as their child's role model. Kind, honest, and fair, all things I value in a person. My best friend, both by the written word and the sense of humor. Every moment of our work was filled with genuine laughter and pure enjoyment. By profession, she is a journalist, but she makes her living playing with social networks, and I can't even start to explain how foreign that is to me. So first of all, I want to thank her for knowing everything I don't because that is what makes us a great team. I am indeed very thankful for her being here for me and with me because if she weren't, my dream would still be just a dream. The way she softens my stubbornness, subdues my anger, and curbs my exuberance, is something I absolutely love and appreciate.

There are many people to whom I would like to say thank you just because they exist in my life. Because they listen to me repeat the same thing hundreds of times, because they believe in me, and because they wish the best for me. There are too many of you to mention you all, but you are all in my heart.

Special thanks to my family. To my dad, who always says: if you don't have the support of your family, you don't have anything. To my brother, who listens to my every insecure "Should I try this? Will it work?" and then answers with "Yes, it will work. Yes, you should try it. Yes. Yes." To my mom, for her selfless love and limitless faith, which makes me who I am, and for absolutely not accepting that there is anyone better than me out there.

The biggest thank you to my husband, Mario. For all the folded laundry, washed dishes, and babysitting so I could finish a chapter in peace. Thank you for the love, understanding, and patience for all my thrills, you are my soulmate. The sweetest thank you goes to my son, for being such a wonderful and good baby. But especially for being, now and forever, my biggest inspiration. I love you, Marino.

And finally, a part in which both of us are saying "thank you" because we are fully aware that without this part, this book would have never happened. First of all, we thank our publisher Ceres, namely our editor Dragutin Dumančić, Ivica Budor, and Marija Drempetić for choosing us, giving us the freedom to do everything precisely as we wished, and making it all possible. You will never know how much that means to us.

We thank Tena Sedlaček, an excellent young architect, for the cover. She took our instructions, which sounded something like this: "We would like it to be really beautiful, like, something striking and stylish, and yet simple and elegant," and designed pure wonder. How she did it, it's beyond our comprehension.

We would also like to thank Andrea Pančur, for reading a thousand versions of one single e-mail because we were in a constant state of panic about looking foolish. She never missed an opportunity to promote our story to anyone and anywhere. She has no idea how many times she saved us.

Special thanks to Alis Marić for giving us our first boost of encouragement that we are actually doing something special. Imagine a person you admire and are almost in awe of them and all that they have achieved. Now imagine that person agreeing to sit down with you and hear your story. And they like it. So much that they share their knowledge with you and direct you, while you are all awkward and confused. Alis Marić was that person for us. We will be grateful to her for the rest of our lives.

First readers' comments

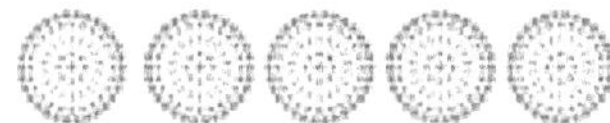

"Fantastic! And that ending?!? I have no words, it's really great!" – *Ružica*

"And just like that, I devoured it… in one sitting. :) I think that says enough. No complaints here." – *Marina (not the author)*

"I can't wait for it to be released, and I'm already sad that I get to read it only once for the first time. :) I love it! I'm so proud, and I want everyone to read this book and be excited about it as we are!" – *Iva*

"I read your book yesterday. It is so beautifully written, both sad and intense at the same time. I can't describe how moved I was by this story. I don't remember the last time something triggered so many emotions in me! Well done!" – *Andrea*

"Beautiful! I can't express how proud I am! It really is a great book, and it would be crazy if it didn't get published. It's amazing!" – *Iva*

"I'm so proud!! Good job, really, I don't have words to praise you enough. I wish you all the luck in the world for this to go the way you imagined it and, once again, well done!" – *Tihana*

"I read it in record time. I doubt I will ever read any of your books again if you don't promise me they won't be as cruel and won't cause a tremendous sadness accompanied by tears as this one did." – *Mario*

"I read it all, it is a very well written, interesting and promising reading. You two have a great connection, I could not always figure out who wrote which chapter." – *Jadranka*

"I don't know is it because I can visualize the surroundings, but it was effortless for me to get into the story. You made me cry, frustrated me, and made me laugh." – *Irena*

"Bravo. In the wake of a trend of modern two-author writing, they appear under the double pseudonym. Two courageous female writers. Interesting. If this is a debut, genuine congratulations." – *Vesna*

"Dear girls, I thank you for the honor of being among the first to read *Leap*. To say I'm impressed would be an understatement!" – *Nataša (again, not the author)*

"It really made me cry, it moved me and encouraged me. I like how anyone can relate to some parts of the story." – *Josipa*

"I am really enjoying this book. You two are wonders!" – *Iva*

"It's very readable. The sentences are short, just the way I like it, so you can't forget what's going on by the end of the sentence." – *Gordana*

"I really like it, I read it in two days. The style and all, it's very fluent." – *Lucija*

"Now I can't wait for the covers so I could read it properly, lying somewhere on a beach. It's straightforward, fluent, readable, and the sentences just flow, which is wonderful!" – *Matea*

"I really liked it. You made me cry and laugh and smile. Well done!" – *Mateja*

"Amazing, amazing! The book really clicked with me, and I look forward to holding it in some more practical format." – *Tena*

Mana Pass

Leap (of faith)

Novel

Put rukopisa

Vinogradska 118

44320 Kutina, Croatia

manapass1010@gmail.com

Contact

+385997981299

+385998331262

Translation

Maja Kulej

Graphic design

Tena Sedlaček